The Heart of Elvis

by

Robynn Gabel

5-12-19

TO THE READER:

HOPE YOU ENJOY
THE JOURNEY WITH
ELVIS.
THANK YOU FOR
READING!

Ralynn Gabel

ROBYNN GABEL

The author copyrights this work of non-fiction in its entirety, and no part shall be used for any purpose without written permission of said author.

The Heart of Elvis

by Robynn Gabel

Createspace Edition.

ISBN-13: 978-1484104279

ISBN-10: 1484104277

Formatting, layout, image processing, cover design and publishing by: Richter Indy Publishing

Photography Credits

Chapter One: *Elvis at age six – 1998*
Photo by R. Gabel

Chapter Two: *Elvis practicing -*
SumPhoto - Circa 2004 –
www.sumphoto.com

Chapter Three: *Chasing cows – 2007 Great Western Celebration*
Richard Griffith –
regriffith1@gmail.com

Chapter Four: *Katelynn whispering to Elvis- 2006 BSFTA Show*
Debbie Hamilton –
debbiekh@montana.com

Chapter Five: *Jaquelynn and Katelynn – 2000*
Photo by R. Gabel

Chapter Six: *Training with Jane – 2004*
Photo by Sonya Murphy

Chapter Seven: *Elvis and I – 2007*
Lucy Knorr – EquuSmile Photography
lucyknorr@equusmile.com

Chapter Eight: *Trail Class – Circa 2004*
Sonya Murphy – SumPhoto –
www.sonyamurphyphotography.com

Chapter Nine: *Jaquelynn and Elvis on a trail ride - 2005*
Photo by R. Gabel

Chapter Ten: *Elvis executing a side pass - 2006 BSFTA Show*
Debbie Hamilton –
debbiekh@montana.com

Chapter Eleven: *Elvis hugging Lochlan, Gavin riding, Trent leading - 2012*
Photo by R. Gabel

Chapter Twelve: *Derick, Trent and Jaquelynn giving Elvis a bath – 2011*
Picturesque Photography –
www.picturesquemt.com

Photography Credits

Chapter Thirteen: *First in Western Pleasure at the GWC – 2006*
Lucy Knorr- EquuSmile Photography –
lucyknorr@equusmile.com

Chapter Fourteen: *Elvis cantering in Reining – 2007*
Richard Griffith –
regriffith1@gmail.com

Chapter Fifteen: *Showmanship – MFTHBA 2007 Show & Celebration*
Fleming Foto – Arlene Portraits - arlenesportraits.com

Chapter Sixteen: *Elvis the character – 2007*
Lucy Knorr – EquuSmile Photography –
lucyknorr@equusmile.com

Chapter Seventeen: *Elvis and Elvis in Costume Class – 2005*
Custom Services Unlimited –
tjamine_@hotmail.com

Chapter Eighteen: *Derick and Elvis – 2011*
Picturesque Photography –
 www.picturesquemt.com

Chapter Nineteen: *Super horses - Circa 2004*
Sonya Murphy - SumPhoto –
www.sumphoto.com

Chapter Twenty: *English Class – 2011*
Picturesque Photography –
www.picturesquemt.com

Chapter Twenty-one: *Mud-caked Elvis – 2012*
Photo by R. Gabel

Epilogue: *2007*
Lucy Knorr – EquuSmile Photography –
lucyknorr@equusmile.com

Cover design by : Rick Carufel
Photo by: Lucy Knorr – EquuSmile Photography
lucyknorr@equusmile.com

ELVIS HAS LEFT THE BARN

Chapter One – In the Beginning

"You want to do what?" I stared at my husband over my cup of coffee.

"Well, we don't have much to do today. I thought we could go look at that horse you were talking about last week," Darrell said, smiling like it was the best idea ever.

Taking a slow sip, I wondered who had actually received the concussion--him or me. I'd just gotten out of the hospital from having the first horse I'd ever owned almost kill me, and looking at another horse was the last thing on my mind.

Two hours later, there I was in dust-filled air heavy with the musty-acrid odor of horses. Tony, the owner of the ugliest horse I'd ever seen, had just finished riding him bareback. He ducked under the horse's neck, petting him all over to prove the little equine was "bomb proof." I decided that Tony was definitely in on my husband's plot, but I didn't want to look at the chunky gelding. Compared to my sleek, sorrel mare, he was broad chested, knobby kneed and an odd combination of colors. As far as I was concerned, he was like any other horse with the standard issue of four legs, head, mane and tail.

"Now, the reason I'm selling him is he can be slow. He's the horse I let people ride when they come to visit, and he's only five. He would be perfect for you--nice and easy. I have to tell you: he doesn't back up and can be pretty heavy on the bit. He's not ever going to be a show horse because he can't fox-trot. He likes the pace too much. The only thing I don't like about him is he can be stubborn. I've had to ride him with spurs sometimes to get him going. But unlike that ornery mare you got, he's just a good ole boy," Tony announced with pride.

He left me with his wife in the corral while he showed Darrell his other horses. I headed for the gate, trying to figure out how to politely tell his wife I wasn't interested. I heard the soft plop of the horse's hooves as he walked up behind me. His breath fanned my neck, and I froze, waiting for a bite or a shove, as my mare was prone to do. Instead, I felt him gently drop his head over my shoulder and pull me back against his chest in a semblance of a horse hug. He snuffled at my pockets, looking for goodies.

I truly didn't want to own a horse again, but what can I say? I changed my opinion about who the lunatic was. I wrote the check out on the spot, and to this day, I don't know what I paid for the little Missouri Fox Trotter called Jake's Elvis J, who had the nickname of Elvis.

I noticed that as I signed Elvis's registration papers, Cindy, Tony's wife, shifted uncomfortably. With a sad look in her eyes, she told me he'd been a therapy horse, was sure-footed on the trail and loved working cows.

"You're going to miss him, aren't you?" I asked.

She nodded. "I've enjoyed riding him, and I can trust him. He can be a little stubborn, as Tony says, but I just hope you're happy with him."

"He will have a great home; I promise," I said solemnly.

We were in-between horse trailers at the time, so I had to leave Elvis behind for a couple of days. I drug my friends down to see him. Marilyn wasn't impressed at all with his looks and wondered about his big knees. Peg, my riding instructor, preferred Quarter

Horses. She thought his stocky build made him look a little like the breed she liked. But I could see in their eyes the same impression I had when I'd first seen him.

The first day home, I led him around to show him his new home. He followed behind me, checking things out. Unlike the mare I had before him, Elvis acted like he wanted to be with me. Sniffing my hands, my face and nickering when I would come out of the house. Elvis had picked me to be his owner, of that I had no doubt.

In buying my first horse, the mare, I made all the mistakes a city girl would. I had picked flashy, fiery and beautiful over calm-minded. The mare was trained and knowledgeable, and more than I could handle. She'd been frustrated by my lack of skill. Before I was bucked off and kicked by her, I had wanted to become a horseman.

That meant having enough experience to ride gracefully and communicate smoothly. The only hitch to this was that Elvis spoke horse--I spoke human. I would have to learn a new language, learn how to ride, and we would have to learn together how to compromise.

Chapter Two – The First Ride

In the early morning light, I hefted the saddle up over Elvis's back, the smell of the new leather wafting in the air. Pulling the stiff cinch leather through the ring, I began to tighten it, and he sucked in air like a blowfish. I didn't think anything of this because I was your classic dude rider. Merriam-Webster defines a "dude" as a city dweller unfamiliar with life on the range. In Wyoming a dude rider is considered someone unfamiliar with the way of horses. I was about to learn my first "dude" lesson.

A couple of friends had invited me to ride out in the high desert. That's what they called the rolling hills, shallow arroyos, cactus and sagebrush in Wyoming. There would also be a wide assortment of wildlife interspersed with cows.

I was nervous about riding with my friends. Would Elvis do as I asked? Could I ride well enough that they wouldn't think I was a beginner? I felt woefully unprepared.

My friends were already saddled and waiting for me. Marilyn was sitting astride a well-proportioned Missouri Fox Trotter mare named Candy. Sally was on an elegant Arabian called Buddy. I so badly wanted to impress them with my new horse.

As I went to mount up, the saddle slipped sideways and I ended up on my butt on the ground. Elvis turned around and looked at me. Both women immediately asked if I was okay. I knew I was very red because I suddenly felt like I was in the pits of Hell. I made a mental note to my dude-self: always check to make sure the cinch is secure before putting weight in the stirrup, and remember Elvis likes to suck in air so I can't get the cinch tight.

I swung a leg over and sat proudly on the new saddle I'd just bought. It had ornate tooling on the leather but was shabbily made. After all, Elvis had to have something that looked good on him. The new leather squeaked and creaked in joyous abandon, but after a while, the noise began to grate on my nerves. Being on a budget, I had bought the cheapest tack I could, but Elvis didn't seem to mind.

"You know, if you put some cornstarch where the leather rubs, it won't squeak. You need to put your heels down," Sally informed me.

Well, so much for impressing anyone. I pulled back on the reins, which applied pressure to the bit in Elvis's mouth. He proved he had no idea what that bar in his mouth had to do with stopping. He kept right on going . . . until I practically had to put my foot on the horn to pull hard enough to stop him. I could see he needed some practice on the human language of "Whoa." I could turn him, but that was the extent of his understanding.

The wide open expanse of prairie dotted with sagebrush stretched endlessly in front of us. The wind whispered encouragement for all to run free. Sally decided to do just that and let her Arabian out at a gallop. I suddenly had a real good sense of what a jockey on a racehorse felt like. Without warning, Elvis sprinted in pursuit of the galloping horse in front of us. It seemed that God had played a trick on Elvis. He'd given him a Fox Trotter's body but a thoroughbred's heart. I stayed on only because I could "monkey clutch" really well. (Wrapping one's legs around the horse and holding onto the saddle horn for dear life.)

Monkey clutching like crazy as he ran away with me, I leaned forward, wrapping an arm around the horn. I lost the stirrups and didn't know where the reins went. As I watched the sagebrush speed by under us, I contemplated bailing because by now I had lost my center of gravity and was bouncing all over the saddle.

As I started to go limp and fall off, he felt the change. He thought his job was to keep the rider on his back, so he'd learned to adjust to keep him or her there. He slowed, shifting to help keep me with him. That's when I found the reins and started slowly applying a one-rein stop, the equivalent of an emergency brake. As we circled down, I was pleased I was back in the center of the saddle. Not so pleased that both of my friends were looking at me with amazement in their eyes. This was probably because I still sat on top of the horse.

I was now beyond embarrassed. Definitely wasn't the sitting-tall-and-looking-cool ride that I had wanted. Turning around to head back to the trailer, I experienced another one of Elvis's quirks. Walking quietly behind the other horses wasn't going to happen. He apparently thought he needed to be in front of everyone. He ignored my pull on the reins once again and ran up behind Marilyn's mare. The rut we were riding in was narrow, so he shouldered them, almost knocking both rider and mare over. The mare froze, clamping down her tail and tucking her butt under her. Since Elvis couldn't stop his forward motion, his chest and leg ended up on top of the mare's rear end. Marilyn's eyes grew large as she glanced over her shoulder to see Elvis riding along behind her.

I got a stern lecture from Marilyn about riding etiquette (as I should have) and a show of pinned ears and a tail swish from her offended mare. When the trailer came into view, there was no stopping Elvis in his gallop to get to it. I was pretty sure that I wouldn't have to worry about being embarrassed ever again while riding with these two ladies because I was positive they weren't going to be inviting me out to ride any time soon.

I was disappointed and frustrated. Where was the nice, quiet horse who'd given me a horse hug? How was I supposed to get this horse to understand what I needed? As I pulled off the saddle, Elvis looked around at me, his liquid-brown eyes hopeful. "Nope, not going to let you suck up," I said with a stern shake of my finger. Stepping in front of him to pick up the lead rope, he leaned his head down, looking hopeless. I folded and gave him a treat, reasoning to myself that I was just a beginning rider. Practice was what we needed.

THE HEART OF ELVIS

Chapter Three – Elvis the Cow Horse

After my first ride, my friends must have decided to keep my public humiliation to themselves, proving they were really friends. I know this because Dick and Jane, friends I knew through church, asked if I could help out on a cattle drive, and they didn't seem aware of my ineptness.

I was so excited. I had wanted to do this ever since I was a little girl. But it was painfully evident that I needed horseback-riding lessons. It was a blow to my pride. I had thought all I needed was natural balance to stay in the saddle. Peg was not only a trainer but gave lessons, so I hired her. She has remained my friend . . . though I don't know why.

"Which front leg is moving out? Call it out to

me," she hollered across the arena.

"Right, left, right, left," I said grumpily.

It wouldn't be until later on, when I'd practiced by myself, that these early lessons would finally make sense. But right then, I was just a forty-year-old teenager with a Godzilla attitude. At least Elvis learned to stop when I asked him to.

I was thinking the horseback lessons had greatly increased my skill, so we could handle the cattle ride. I knew Elvis had worked cows before. I was sure we would make up for our first bumbling effort and wow everyone with our teamwork. I was riding with seasoned riders, and once again I only thought about my reputation as a horseman. Growing up as a city girl, all I knew about ranching was what I'd seen in the movies.

In the brisk morning air, the horses trotted out quickly towards the herd, wanting to run, but their riders held them back. I was nervous. I could barely manage a walk, let alone a trot. I made the mistake of trying to slow Elvis down.

Suddenly his head went down, and I felt his back end rise up and his hind feet kick out. I shrieked, "Knock it off, Elvis!" It's a good thing that he wasn't very athletic and didn't put a lot of effort into his bucking because after a few crow-hops, I was ready to call it quits. I didn't know it at the time, but the often-repeated phrase I had hollered at him would become our trademark among our friends.

As we trailed behind the cows, I noticed he was acknowledging the bit and slowing, but he had a new trick under his saddle. Suddenly, he grabbed the bit between his teeth and flipped his nose up, pulling the reins out of my hands. Then, he dropped his head and grabbed a mouthful of grass.

Marilyn joked, "Hey, don't you feed him?"

The look I gave her must have been homicidal because she moved her horse off quickly.

Elvis had his druthers about being behind stinky, slow-moving cows. I must admit that I did also. (The only thing a cow is good for, in my opinion, is to lay on a plate and be medium rare.) To speed them up, he'd reach out and bite their butts, impatient at their sluggish pace. This wasn't acceptable behavior from a cow horse, so I reined him to the outside of the herd. He pranced, wanting to move. At last, with aching arms, I conceded to his superior strength. I asked Dick if I could just lead them in. A strange look crossed his face. "Uh, well, I guess so," he said.

Striding out proudly, Elvis led those wayward cows home. On the way back, I knew one thing for sure. Tony, Elvis's previous owner, had been very wrong: Elvis wasn't slow. Later on, after learning something about how one moves cows and the finer points of how to "push" the herd, I would come to understand Dick's confusion. One does not lead a cow anywhere!

Yet, my dear friends continued to call and invite me on cattle drives. This was either sheer Christian charity on their part, or desperation. I never could figure out which.

Each time we helped on a cattle drive, I noticed

that our communication got a little better. Elvis also knew how to do things I was not aware of, like rollbacks. If you are following a cow off its hip and it suddenly stops and turns around and heads in the other direction (and believe me, this is done at lightning speed), your horse is supposed to do the same thing.

There's always one stubborn cow in the bunch, wanting to go in a different direction than the rest of them. On this ride, we had searched out cows through sagebrush, and over hill and dale. We had about fifty head altogether; we pushed them all towards the gate. One rangy, red cow decided to run up the fence line, away from the gate, and Dick hollered for me to go get her.

Elvis was up for the chase. We were right off her left hip, trying to get ahead and stop her to turn her back. I could tell this was a cow that had been chased before. Without warning, she stopped and turned. One minute I was going west--the next instant, east. I felt like a cartoon character, hanging in midair, saying, "Where did the horse go?" Luckily, I actually stayed in the saddle, but I had no idea Elvis was that supple.

During all these cattle rides of shame, Dick gave me hope. "Elvis seems like he's a cowy horse. He really likes bossing those cows."

"Cowy" is an expression used to describe a horse that seems to have a natural ability to work a cow. The horse will watch them and seem to know where they are going to head or where they may be hiding in the draws and valleys.

But for all his savvy ways, Elvis's need for

speed at last got him into trouble. I loaned him out on several occasions to Dick. On this ride, Dick and Elvis had to cross a river after a stray cow. Elvis was doing his usual hurrying along and ran into a bog. Close to the river are low-lying areas that look deceptively solid but are actually waterlogged clay.

Elvis sunk to his chest, totally mired. Dick had to crawl off and then coax him to scramble out. A lot of horses would panic, thrashing and miring themselves deeper, and become exhausted. Dick was very impressed with Elvis's calmness. He worked on pulling his legs out, then rested, then worked, then rested, until he finally got out.

A few weeks later during a leisurely stroll behind a herd of cattle, I received one of my best horsemanship lessons. The dust rose around the cows as they plodded along. Little flies hung around back ends, sloppy with cow-pie remnants, while long streams of spittle ran from moist noses. We slowly pushed them along and chatted with our fellow riders. I watched with jealousy as Charlie rode Elvis. I was riding a young palomino-colored Fox Trotter gelding I had been given. He was in training and this was Nugget's first cattle ride. We'd been struggling in our communication.

Charlie was the quintessential modern cowboy. Having grown up with horses and livestock, he'd learned how to quietly communicate with a horse. Charlie and Elvis easily found cows in timber, gulches and prairie, and patiently guided them towards the home gates. Where I would have had to yank, pull or slow Elvis down, calmly, he worked from Charlie's unseen cues, cutting, pushing and rounding up the wayward cows.

We stopped for the noon break. I watched Charlie break out his lunch, which included a big red apple. With the pocket knife no self-respecting cowboy would be without, he cut it up. Elvis's head came up from grazing, and he sniffed inquisitively in Charlie's direction. He chuckled and gave Elvis a few slices and then the core, all of which Elvis munched on happily. I had no idea Elvis even liked apples.

"So how did you know he'd eat an apple?"

"Tony was my neighbor. When Elvis came to live with him, that little colt was quite the Houdini of gates. He was always escaping. Horses usually love apples, can smell them a ways off too. All I had to do was go out with a cut-up apple and he'd come right to me."

"I wish I could get Elvis to do half of what he does for you," I said, a hint of irritation in my voice.

Charlie's sun-leathered, wrinkled face was split by a smile. "Old Elvis here, he knows what to do. I just let him do his job. Sometimes I have to give him a little direction and sometimes I have to get after him. He might want to argue, but he is a good boy. You just give him his head. Only pick up the reins when you want him to do something."

"Really? If I don't slow him down, we're running all over the place," I complained.

He reached up to stroke Elvis's neck. "You do that, old boy? Are you being ornery? You need to listen to the little lady." He chuckled. "Just relax and trust your horse. But I've watched you and Elvis. He likes you. I think he'd do anything for you." He went on about how his father had taught him to ride, and his most prized possession, his saddle, was on Elvis's back.

I wasn't sure if Charlie was right. I thought Elvis only liked me for the treats he could get out of me. But I knew one thing for sure: I wanted to ride Elvis as well as Charlie did.

After years of cattle rides, we eventually worked out a partnership. Charlie was right: I had to just trust Elvis and stay off the reins. I would guide and direct, but when it came to finding the cows and moving them, he was in charge. He proved his cow sense more than once. Like the time when the five cows we were trying to push to the gate broke away and crossed the river. Then they split. Three went up a hill, and the other two went around the side of the hill.

I thought this was going to be a lot of work, especially since we couldn't split in half. I figured three cows were better than two. I guided him towards the hill, but Elvis nosed out on the reins, so I gave him some slack. Instead of going up the hill, he went after the two on the bottom. I figured it was just Elvis being lazy. But instead, as we pushed the two out and back into the river, the three who had been watching at the top of the hill got worried when their buddies headed off in a different direction without them. Sure enough, down came the other three to join them.

I had to retire Elvis from chasing cows finally,

as he developed a navicular bone problem in his right hoof and couldn't turn quick enough without hurting. On his last cow roundup, I informed the riders we had ridden with for several years that it would be our last.

"Ahh, that's too bad," Dick told me.

I was touched. I just knew it was because my horsemanship had improved so much, or Elvis had impressed them with his cow sense. But then he finished, saying, "We are going to miss the rodeo every spring, and you hollering 'Knock it off, Elvis!'"

Chapter Four - Trusting One Another

At first, I only had one horse, but within a couple weeks after purchasing Elvis, I suddenly had three. I traded my first horse, the mare, to a breeder for a runt, coffee-colored Fox Trotter yearling mare. I was also given a palomino-colored colt that my mare had given birth to in the spring.

In every relationship, trust must be established. This was the same for the new horses. I had to teach the youngsters how to lead on halter, load into the trailer, be able to have their feet trimmed and in general trust us to handle them. In the next months, I found I could also trust Elvis.

Since I was still learning about tack, equipment and horses in general, we went through several used horse trailers. The first decent one I had was a used Stidham that had two forward-facing travel chutes. The hitch had a collar on the ball clamp that had to be pushed forward to lock the clamp into place.

Elvis happily loaded right into the horse trailer on a bright spring day, as he hadn't been out of the pasture for a few weeks. Closing the tailgate behind him, I slid open the feeder window so he could get some fresh air. Walking back up front, I checked the collar one more time. It had a tendency to stick and not lock--something I had mentioned to my husband several times. It seemed snug, but just to make sure, I gave it a little kick. Nothing shifted.

Because of the very busy highway we lived next to, I would have to give it a little gas and pull out quickly. Unfortunately, there was a dip where our graveled road met the pavement, and it could pop the hitch off a trailer pull.

As I gunned it, I felt a sickening lurch. I slammed on the brakes and glanced in the rearview mirror in time to see the trailer heading to the right. The emergency chains now caught the runaway trailer and the back end of the SUV did another jerk. I froze.

After applying the emergency brake, I jumped out, my stomach in knots. The hitch now rested down in the barrow ditch; the trailer had tipped forward, tilting the back gate almost three feet off the ground. My horse was in there!

I frantically called my husband on my cell phone, and I won't repeat his uncharacteristic reply to my frantic explanation. In the edited version, it went something like this: "What! You didn't check the collar, did you? It wasn't locked; that's the only way this could have happened! I'm at work, and you're going to need to jack up that front end and there's no jack out there. Was there any damage to the SUV? How the heck did this happen . . . ?" and on and on.

As the debate raged over his imagined negligence on my part, I thought of Elvis. There was no movement, no kicking, nothing. I thought I had killed him, and dreaded opening the back door to the trailer.

Click! I slammed the phone shut. Tears blurred my vision, and breathing was getting harder. I was obviously on my own. Gingerly, I lifted the latch, imagining the worst. Elvis's chest was pressed up against the trailer wall, his head in the feed compartment in front of him. I always looped a lead rope up over his neck, and it was still in place, but I couldn't reach it. I grabbed his tail, his butt too high in the air for me to tap, and I started to gently tug, while standing way back to avoid a panicked kick.

This would be the tricky part. Even the most

athletic horse has a hard time with the first step down, and that is usually only a foot off the ground. This drop was almost three feet. He could injure a back leg easily by scraping it or going under the trailer and banging his hock.

My horses were always trained to understand voice commands, as I talked to them constantly. Using the same commands over and over, they learned what action I wanted. Now, I spoke quietly, "Back, Elvis. Back." He shuffled backwards methodically until his back feet got to the lip of the trailer. I tugged on the tail, encouraging him. "Down, Elvis. Down."

Carefully, his back foot came out, searching for the ground. At this point, I trusted he wasn't going to kick me, so I stood to the side and grabbed his leg, helping to guide it down. He pulled it back several times, not feeling anything solid where it should have been. Finally, he lowered his hind end down while finally trusting me to guide his left foot to the ground.

It was amazing. Once the hind foot hit the ground, he kicked out the other one to join it. His belly almost touched the floor as he started pushing off against the slanted surface. Finally, his front half was out, all four feet on the ground. He turned his head to give me a famous Elvis look. I could almost see the "what was all of that about" in his eyes. I loved on him, feeding him goodies.

I had just put him back in the corral when my husband turned onto the shoulder of the road and went to work jacking up the trailer so I could maneuver the SUV into place to re-hitch the trailer. Again, I stubbornly explained that I had checked the hitch and it was locked. Period.

A few weeks later (Because he wouldn't let me hitch it up, he had to do it now), I was watching him as he drove out the trailer for me to load up with. When the trailer hit a pothole in our gravel driveway, once again the hitch popped off the ball, landing it in the gravel.

He jumped out of the SUV, cussing. Again, I will edit. "What the heck? But I checked that lock! It has to be sticking because I know I checked it!" Darrell stomped around for a few more minutes, repeating his frustrations. I just stood there. I didn't say a word, proving my great love for him.

In the first few years that we owned Elvis, he led a rather eventful life as we all learned different things about horsemanship. After I acquired the young horses, Elvis was my only rideable horse. My friend, Ben, the owner of the stud that had bred my first mare, offered to loan me a Fox Trotter mare he was sure would change my mind about the fairer sex of the horse world. Her name was Cameo.

I was excited because this meant I would now have two broke horses, so my husband could ride with me for the first time. We decided not to go far, just up the little country road that was across from us. The only problem: we had to cross the very busy highway that ran in front of our property.

It was a beautiful spring day, birds chirping, with a slight breeze and a cloud-free sky. I saddled up quickly, while Darrell took a quick tug on Elvis's cinch. I knew Elvis would "take care" of my less experienced husband, which really boiled down to the blind leading the blind.

I loved the kind nature of the mare I was riding, but I still fancied geldings. Nothing could override my prejudice after the accident with my first horse. I mounted and watched my husband heave himself up on Elvis. The gray gelding turned around and sniffed at his shoe, eyeing his new victim. Looking back at me and the little mare I was on, Elvis pinned back his ears. He didn't like it when I rode another horse.

Off we went, leather squeaking, the clop of the horses' feet giving a soothing rhythm to the ride. Slowly, we crossed the asphalt; it can be quite slick under four hooves. I watched Elvis as he picked his way carefully. I must admit I enjoyed watching him more than riding him at times.

The gentle sway of the mare's cadence again reminded me of why I loved riding a gaited versus a non-gaited horse. Several times, Elvis moved over next to my mare and shouldered into her, swinging his head with his ears pinned, like he might bite her. Obviously, she was used to grumpy male horses and easily stepped out of the way. They got along fine in the pasture, but he wanted to make sure she knew he was still the boss, even if I rode her.

The rest of the ride was uneventful, except for the occasional admonishment from my husband to Elvis to speed it up. Elvis usually took his time with a new rider, checking out what they knew.

As we crossed the busy road to go home, we

decided to hustle a little. A big rig was coming towards us faster than we'd thought. Darrell kicked Elvis to hurry him along, and suddenly I heard him shout at me. I turned in my saddle to see my husband hanging sideways. Now it was a full-blown panic situation.

"Just let go and fall off! Hurry!" I hollered.

With an "ugh" and a soft thud, he hit the road, the trucker now honking. I leaped off my mare, grabbing her reins as well as Elvis's as my husband scrambled off the road. Elvis had stood very still during the ungraceful dismount. The saddle hung under his belly, and I was waiting for him to balk or go into a buck. Instead, very carefully, as if walking on hot coals, he minced to the side of the road just as a whoosh of air from the diesel rig hit us.

Back at the barn, we marveled over the little gray, feeding him goodies. Darrell learned, as I had, to always double check Elvis's cinch.

To build trust with all of my new horses, I worked with them from the ground first, using the round pen Darrell built for me. I would send them away from me--what we call to "lunge" them--on a long lead rope. You then get them to circle you. While doing this you can teach them to turn, stop, back up and move in different gaits. I felt if I couldn't get them to respect me from the ground, I certainly wouldn't get it in the saddle, due to my inexperience. I worked with Elvis also, and he caught on quickly to my cues. His trust in my husband and I continued to grow.

It had snowed early that month and a deep freeze had set in. For over four weeks, it had been below zero every night. The snow had lumped into various forms of ice. At night we penned the horses in the corrals up front so we could feed them easier. Darrell complained often that Elvis did not eat to live; he lived to eat.

We had a long, shallow feeder for hay. It was low to the ground and about as wide as the side of a horse. The horses had an irritating habit of nosing out the grass to get to what is called the "fines" or the rich crumbs that had seeds. Then, later, they would clean up around the feeder.

Darrell had lost most of his hearing in his right ear due to tuning up race cars. He slept on his left side, effectively taking out the hearing in that ear at night as well. So to this day I have no idea how he heard the commotion outside, but he did.

Around one o'clock in the morning, I was shaken awake. "Honey, come on. I think Elvis is in trouble." I stumbled after him, wondering what trouble three horses could possibly get into within a paneled enclosure. When we got outside, it was already twenty-below zero. There in the shallow feed trough, on his side, lay Elvis. The width of the feeder was just wide enough that his whole left side was wedged into it. I immediately put a halter on his head and pulled with all my might. He thrashed, trying to get out, but his legs were useless as they hung off the side, not touching the ground. Elvis's breathing was labored; his weight was suffocating him. We would have to hustle.

As we stood, looking at the predicament he had got himself into, I could see no way around it. We would have to attach a chain to either side of the feeding trough and tip it over on its side to free him. The chain would form a V from the hitch to the legs of the feeder. There would be just enough room for a horse to stand in between, but if he thrashed on the way over, he could destroy the back of the pickup and injure himself.

I hoped Elvis would be his usual levelheaded self. I leaned over, and in one fuzzy ear, I told him he would have to trust us. We would help him. He needed to just stay calm.

My husband is into cars like I'm into horses. Keeping them shiny, running well and dent free has always been a source of pride. He had just bought a brand new truck that we were going to have to use to save Elvis. Now he backed it up to the feeder without hesitation, proving his great love for me.

Quickly, the chains were attached. Darrell hopped into the truck and slowly took off while I held onto the rope, which was attached Elvis's halter, to help stabilize him and hopefully prevent him from thrashing again. Slowly, the feeder tipped over on its side, and a very grateful Elvis lay where he'd been spilled out between the two chains. We waited, holding our breath, until he gathered his feet under himself, heaved up, stood unmoving between the chains and caught his breath while we scrambled to unhitch.

It was obvious there was trust on both sides of the fence now

THE HEART OF ELVIS

Chapter Five – Kids and Elvis

As I worked at trying to learn better horsemanship, I observed other things about Elvis. It was evident right away he loved kids. He showed me in encounter after encounter that he had a gentle soul that understood them. Elvis could always depend on a handful of grass offered by grubby, little hands. Sometimes, he'd even get a horse treat if the kid knew where they were kept. When Elvis came to my home, grandkids were already making their appearance in the world. Having sixteen grandkids and their various friends always visiting, my horses learned right away that kids were a good thing.

The grandchildren liked coming to our house since it was twenty acres of room to roam and had cool things like four-wheelers. And I know they loved seeing us, their grandparents, as well. But I had a sneaking suspicion that getting to pet, feed and ride the horses was at the top of their have-fun list.

Even though I lectured, warned and growled, not all of them would listen to my dire warnings of not going into the corral to pet the horses. From the fence was okay, but I knew that even the best of horses, if startled, could trample a small child underfoot.

Elvis was always the first to greet the happy kids and reap the benefits of their need to feed the horses. I have always wondered why he didn't take advantage of their lack of horse knowledge as he would with an adult. He treated them fairly, with patience, and took great care not to hurt them.

I remember the first time I encountered a child in the corral: it was a Kodak moment visually, a heart attack physically. My oldest granddaughter, Jaquelynn, all of four-years old, climbed in with Elvis. She happily wrapped her arms around his front legs, her head between his knees, and smiled endearingly at me.

Elvis arched his neck, looking down curiously, while standing statue still. I quietly went into the enclosure and slid my hand down his shoulder while reaching to disengage the giggling girl. When she was extricated and I had her safely in my arms, I leaned into him, resting my head on his neck in gratitude for his calmness. He nuzzled the little girl, looking for his reward.

He gave horsey-back rides freely. I discovered I could depend on him to be patient and gentle in giving an eager toddler a ride around the corral. I always did this bareback and they would hold on to his mane. He would step carefully, balancing them on his broad back.

It was one of those cloudless, blue sky days in Wyoming when my second oldest granddaughter, Katelynn, came to visit. She was still in diapers, but she wanted to ride. I went and got a halter and lead rope for Elvis. Her mom and I set her up on his back. With chubby little hands, she clutched his mane; her blue eyes were alight with joy and fearlessness.

"Go faster. Please, go faster," she pleaded. So I tugged on his lead rope, the signal to step up his speed. He hesitated, sensing her inability to stay on, but being obedient, he went into a rough trot. The bounce was too much for the laughing toddler, and she slipped from his back before we could catch her. She landed on her diapered bottom, sitting up, surprised. Then, she threw herself back on the ground and started to wail.

Elvis turned his head, ears pricked forward, listening to her cries. It was hard for me not to laugh.

Katelynn was tough on the outside, but on the inside, if her feelings were hurt, she could become a puddle of tears in a second. Her mother scooped her up, dusted off her little bottom and reassured her. She reached for the inquisitive nose that Elvis offered, wiping her crocodile tears on the soft end of it. Then, like a cloud revealing the sun, her smile broke free, and she begged to ride once again.

We slid her up on his back, and I asked him to walk out again. This time, he acted as if he was walking on eggshells. Each step was balanced as he adjusted to her squirming and kept her on his back.

"Faster, please, Grandma," she pleaded.

Laughing, I said, "Okay, but no tears if you fall off again. Hold on tight." I tried a tug to speed him up a hair, but he refused. Methodically plodding along, he knew what was best for his bouncing charge. He had a tender heart and remembered her cries. I couldn't have dragged that horse into a trot.

I came to respect and appreciate his innate ability to assess his rider. Later on, as the grandkids grew old enough to ride on their own, I would use his instinct of a rider's skill to determine what other horse in my herd the child could handle. He became my best tool in teaching the children. If they didn't have the skill level to make him do what he needed to do, he would quietly head to the gate and stand there, refusing to go anywhere as they squirmed, kicked and yelled. All my grandkids learned that they couldn't ride any other horse until they could work with Elvis and get him to listen to their cues.

Throughout the years of learning for both of us, I could depend on one thing: Elvis would take care of the children. One 4th of July, I had sixteen grandkids and ten adults over for dinner and a fireworks display. This one was especially fun, as the kids had participated in the annual parade. I didn't notice during the hubbub of family and good food--we were one child short.

I was putting dishes in the dishwasher when my oldest daughter asked, "Mom, have you seen Lindynn?"

"No, but you know how crazy she is about the horses. She's probably out there feeding them hay through the fence," I told her. My daughter headed out the door to check on her youngest child.

I knew something was up when the house phone rang at the same time that my cell went off, and then I heard shouting outside. The breathless voice of my panicked daughter informed me that Lindynn was on Elvis.

"What? There's no way she could get up on him." I clicked my phone shut, thinking again that there was no way a three-year old had climbed up on that horse. I rushed outside and noted all of the family lined up outside the corral panels, no one saying anything, as if any sound might spook Elvis.

We had brought the horses in for the night because the noise of firecrackers might have caused them to go through the wire fence we had around the pasture. Elvis was in his own pen in the back. Since we lived next to a busy road, the night pen was built out of five-foot high cattle panels.

As I went into the corral, Elvis came around the loafing shed, stepping carefully. Lindynn was perched on his back and holding onto his mane. She took one look at my ashen face and immediately started saying, "I'm sorry, Grandma. I'm sorry."

Earlier in the day, during the parade in town, I had put Lindynn up on Elvis's back briefly for a ride. She knew she hadn't asked for permission. Elvis walked up to me, nudging me with his nose as if to say, "I gave her a horsey ride. Where's my treat?" As I slid her off his back, I asked again, "How did you get up on him?"

I got a classic kid answer. "I don't know," she said with a shrug.

Elvis got treats from all the relieved adults. I was so grateful she had not done this with any of the other horses. To this day, all we can figure out is that she had climbed the panels and Elvis had obligingly sidled up to the fence so she could climb on, knowing there was a reward in it for him.

The time that Elvis definitely deserved the title of "saint" was when my grandson, Milton, visited. In his toddler years, he was quite active. My house was always full of grandkids coming and going, so it was easy for Milton to slip into the forbidden corral with the stick he had picked up in his play. I will never know what it is with boys who have to wander around with a stick in their hands.

I was in the house and happened to look out the dining-room window. As a city girl, I had only thought of how wonderful it would be to have the main corral as my view from the front of my house. I didn't realize that view came with a smell!

That view revealed Milton toddling towards a dozing Elvis, who was relaxing in the warm sunshine, letting everything hang out. Realizing where Milton was heading with that stick, I sprinted out the front door at lightning speed. I felt like I was in one of those dreams where you watch in horror as a scene plays out, yet cannot move fast enough to intervene. Milton was short enough to fit under Elvis's belly, and, with a batter's practiced eye, he aimed for the dangling appendage. Even as I hollered, he swung.

Never in my life have I seen a horse suck up so fast. His belly went to his backbone, his eyes popped open wide, and the dangling remnant of his male-hood disappeared. He locked his legs, somehow, even in his half-awake stage, sensing there was a child underneath him. Milton's giggle floated on the air. I was faint from holding my breath, and Elvis slowly turned his regal head to stare at the little juvenile delinquent under his belly.

I wish I could take these Kodak moments frozen in my memory and download them to my computer. The expression on that horse's face would have won many a photo contest! Milton toddled out and headed to my next horse, but by that time, I had finally reached the corral and scooped up the little offender. Elvis politely sniffed him, and I would have given anything to be able to read his mind.

It seemed to me that kids were just naturals at

being able to communicate with animals. I often wished it could have been that simple between Elvis and me.

Chapter Six - To Trail or Not to Trail

I watched in fascination as Peg danced with Nugget, my young, palomino Missouri Fox Trotter. Around each obstacle they flowed, rider and horse as one. You could see no cue. It was as if the horse and rider had one mind. She seemed to think it, and his feet moved to do it. Over the bridge, they moved confidently, side passed over the log, backed up between the logs, weaved between the poles and finally opened and exited the gate. As she came out, I realized I had been holding my breath. Suddenly, I knew she had set the standard for my horsemanship. That was how I wanted to ride my horse. It did not surprise me when she was presented with the first-place ribbon.

I'd come to this little horse show in Powell, Wyoming at the suggestion of several friends. I was in horse heaven. We camped and talked horses with the other contestants for three days. I decided to enter Nugget to give him the exposure. Peg, who had worked so hard on training him, would have a chance to show off what she had accomplished.

With every class she participated in, she wowed me and others with her skill and the ribbons she collected. On the way home, my mind was working overtime. Nugget was more horse than I could handle. Already, I had plans of selling him.

Again frustrated in my horse journey, I'd fought to learn how to ride Nugget to erase the feeling of failure in the encounter with his mother. Though able to ride him, I didn't trust him. Peg and he had a communication that was so much better than what I could convey to him. I knew what I wanted to do: to ride and win a Trail Class. That would mean learning a refined language with a horse, and would surely prove I had become a horseman.

The horse that kept popping into my head was…Elvis. I trusted Elvis. During the ride back home, I turned to Peg and innocently asked, "So do you think that Elvis and I could ever do Trail?" She snorted, glanced over at me and must have read the hope plastered all over my face.

"Look, you'd have to teach him how to canter,

take off in the correct lead, fox-trot and transition between his gaits. He is so stiff I don't think he can do it. Besides, you would have to have very finite moves to be able to negotiate a Trail pattern. Keep working with Nugget; it might take a couple of years, but look how far you've already come. I'm sorry, but Elvis will never make a competitive Trail horse."

Rebelliously, I thought she sounded just like Tony, Elvis's previous owner. At times, it seemed no one saw Elvis as anything more than a horse that was stubborn, slow and tuned out to the load on his back. I had dealt with his intelligence firsthand, seen his fire, his heart and felt the competitive spirit under that hide. I believed he was the little horse that could, and if I'd learn to ride well enough, he'd get a chance to show them the great show horse he could be.

A few months back, while attending a "Learn the Gaits of a Fox Trotter" riding clinic in my hometown, I had met a gaited-horse trainer. She had seemed interested in Elvis. Jane happened to be at the Powell show, so I talked with her and I asked her if she believed in a "heart connection" between owner and horse. Jane and Peg had a very lively debate about it. Peg believed a horse saw us only as a food source and reacted accordingly. No emotion involved. Jane believed that just like some humans couldn't work together, horses and humans had to find their "match" and indeed there could be a heart connection. But best of all, she knew about gait. I lived in Quarter-Horse country, where not many people know about how a Fox Trotter was supposed to move.

So I called her when I got home from the show. "Hi, Jane. Do you remember me? I'm the owner of Elvis."

"Oh, yes, I remember Elvis."

She responded like a typical horse person. They were more likely to remember your horse's name than your name.

I continued. "Well, I have this crazy idea, Jane. I would like you to take Elvis and work with him. And if you think that he will be able to learn a fox-trot, then I'm thinking of working with him and trying my hand at a show and doing Trail Class. But my trainer here, Peg, doesn't think he can do Trail. So I'm looking for a second opinion, if you are willing to do it."

She agreed but warned me that it might take more than a couple of weeks. I agreed to let her try, unless she thought it was hopeless. I would have to take Elvis to her in Powell. As I left him, he whinnied after me, and I felt like I was leaving a child behind.

Two weeks later, I received a call from Jane, asking if I could come up. I pressed her for information. Would he be able to do it? Had she been able to get him to fox-trot? All she would say is that I needed to come up.

My husband came along, I think, to be supportive for the devastating news he thought I was going to receive. As we walked down the long corridor leading to the holding corral in the barn, we were talking. A sudden whinny split the air. Elvis had heard our voices. He was definitely happy to see us. Even Jane smiled at his excitement.

She sent us to the arena as she tacked up. "I will ride him out, and you need to tell me what you think."

I nervously plowed through the loose dirt to wait in the center. Out she came. I seriously had to look twice. Had she changed horses? Surely, this couldn't be Elvis. Instead of my pokey little gray,--who used to change gears, pull on the bit and act unruly--out came a trotting, head shaking, tail swishing, beauty of a horse.

I stared. Where had this horse come from? His stride and rhythm were beautiful. His presence had a spark. This wasn't a horse that was just moving to move. Elvis enjoyed it. He was showing off. My husband just grinned. Even he could see it and he wasn't a horse person.

"So what do you think? Can he fox-trot?" A huge smile showed all of Jane's perfect teeth.

"Oh!" I clapped my hands in glee like a small child.

"I think you have a horse who could do a Trail Class," Jane announced in confidence.

Years later, Jane told me that Elvis was one of the easiest horses she had ever worked with. It was as if he suddenly understood he was a Fox Trotter and fell into the gait quickly. I have always thought it was because he finally had someone that spoke his language and helped him find it. Either way, I knew I had been right. He was talented. It was now my turn to step up and learn how to become a rider, instead of just a passenger.

THE HEART OF ELVIS

Chapter Seven – Making the Connection

The sun was shining outside while the dust rose inside the arena. Peg's voice carried clearly as she again instructed me. "Keep his shoulder in; he's running through it."

I gritted my teeth. The gate was a major attraction to Elvis. As we would come around the arena and go by it, Elvis would turn his head in response to the reins yet still move his shoulder to the gate. I had gone around the arena for the millionth time, it seemed, and I despaired of Elvis getting better.

He was stiff, not wanting to bend easily into the basic circles. I felt I would never be able to keep my shoulders back, heels down, look ahead, cue with my legs and keep him between the reins all at once. It seemed more than my brain could orchestrate at one time.

Now, with my decision to do Trail since Elvis could fox-trot, I'd hired Peg to help me learn how to turn on the hindquarters, turn on the forehand, side pass, slide to a stop, rollback and back up. I didn't tell her my plans for showing, just that I needed help. I hoped to surprise her with a ribbon, proving that she was wrong about Elvis. When she agreed to help me, I naively thought she would teach the horse, and all I'd have to do is sit there and give cues. It was a little more complicated than that.

Rubbing my face, I felt the grit of arena dust. Frustrated, I decided to trot him. As he picked up and we headed into a circle at the far end of the arena, he tripped, going down to his knees, rolling over to his right shoulder and trapping my right ankle in the stirrup under his full weight. He pulled up immediately when I hollered. Of course it was the ankle that I had broken only five months earlier while coming off a hay stack. As I lay rolling in the dirt in pain, he moved closer, his head down, snuffling at me, and stood by my side.

Another rider had been working a young horse in the arena, as well as Peg. He rode up and jumped off his horse.

"Are you okay?" His dark eyes looked me over quickly.

"Give me a few seconds," I said, gingerly testing my weight on the injured ankle. He turned to look at Elvis's face.

When he was younger, Elvis's color had been black with scattered sorrel, and he had a star in the middle of his forehead. People would ask me what color he was, and I would always ask them what color they thought he was. They'd chuckle, and I had heard everything from roan to gray. As he grew older, the black gave way to gray, leaving half his face a sorrel-and-black mixed marking. I thought it fit his two-sided nature quite well.

"What's your horse's name?" I was getting used to this in the horse world. "Elvis. Why?"

He reached out to run his hand down the horse's forehead. Elvis responded by nosing at his hand. "I broke this horse when Tony owned him. He's quite the cow horse, and can be stubborn as hell. He liked to race too. We had to rope him and take his feet out from under him a few times, but he learned not to run away."

I knew my eyes grew large at his statement. He patted him again. "He was one of my favorites. He's a good horse. Obviously, he likes you."

"Why do you say that?"

"He didn't head to the gate like he normally does, and just stood here beside you."

We chatted for a few more moments; then, I

limped off to unsaddle. Now I had an answer to a couple of things. Elvis got nervous and hated ropes around him or his feet. Snorting and sidling sideways if a rope came near him. And there was a connection between this horse and I that wasn't totally based on horse treats.

By now my little herd had grown to four Missouri Fox Trotters. I would practice in the ring with Elvis and try to apply the horsemanship skills I was learning with him to my younger horses. I was discouraged at how slow it seemed to be going. It was even more frustrating for Elvis. He had to babysit anyone who visited and wanted to ride during that time.

I received my horse-crazy gene through a long line of ancestors. It came down from my grandfather, to my mother, to me. So when she came for one of her rare visits, the first place my mother headed to was the horses, offering them a handful of hay. Now in her late sixties, I knew she hadn't been on a horse in over twenty years. Elvis, I decided, would be just the horse for her to ride, and I helped her to crawl up on his broad back. He turned patiently to sniff her shoe, trying to get to know this new rider, and then he looked at me with eyes that said, "Really? Another one?" He balked at moving out, and I found this odd. Usually he was compliant and willing.

It was a summer that was unusually busy for us. Just a week later, my brother-in-law visited. He had ridden throughout his life and was a confident rider. I gave him Elvis to ride, as I needed to work my young palomino-colored gelding, Nugget.

He swung into the saddle, and Elvis didn't do his usual sniffing of the rider's shoe. In fact, he swished his tail irritably as we moved out. A few moments down the trail, my brother-in-law began to have problems. Elvis didn't seem to like him. He ran through the reins, ducked his head to eat, swished at his rider with his tail and finally crow-hopped. I had learned this meant Elvis was putting his hoof down.

"I'm so sorry, Terry. He's never done this before!" Now I was in a dilemma. Could I trust Nugget, who was still in training, to work with Terry? But I had no choice. Elvis was snorting and looking rebellious. Trading horses, I got up on Elvis, expecting fireworks. Instead he happily turned to sniff my shoe, and then moved off in a breathtaking flatfoot walk. No sign of irritation anywhere.

Terry was relieved; Nugget moved out with a soft stride, happily working with him.

What had just happened? Was it Terry? Had Elvis just decided he had found someone he didn't like? Maybe it was because he didn't like men. No, that couldn't be; he'd never done this with Darrell, my husband.

I was about to get my answer. I went back to riding Elvis, thinking he needed a refresher course on the cues. A horse will go to the level of his rider, and he'd been getting away with a lot lately. My friend Marilyn called and asked me to play hooky from church with her, and go for a ride in the desert.

On a sunny August morning, with the sky a

blue vault overhead, we headed out in a brisk flatfoot walk. I'd been working on cuing Elvis to pick up a canter. So with soft pressure from my right calf against his side, he easily went into a canter. As we came around a corner, I suddenly went flying through the air, crashing down onto my right hip. Hitting hard, the breath knocked from me, I saw a brief flash of Elvis rolling over onto his side.

Just like us, a horse can trip. Going full speed, four legs are easily tangled. As I lay moaning on the ground, Elvis came to stand next to me, while Marilyn raced to us. From the tip of his nose to almost his forelock, Elvis had scraped the skin off because he had used his face to stop himself. I struggled to my feet, using the stirrup to grab onto. He stood rock still.

"Are you okay?" Marilyn asked breathlessly.

"No. I don't know if I can walk," I replied.

She had parked the pickup and horse trailer up on the hill. A very rough road wound its way down to where we were, but I wasn't sure if she could get to me with it. Cell service was spotty and it was important I get back to town right away. I took a few steps, and pain shot from my lower back all the way down through my ankle. Moaning, I leaned against Elvis's shoulder. I could move, but each step was going to hurt. Looking at Elvis's face close-up, I started to cry. It was bleeding now and would have to be doctored.

"I'm going to try and go get the truck. You might have fractured something," she said.

"Okay. I will wait for you."

She rode off, heading up the hill. It would take

her about twenty minutes to get to the trailer and who knew how long to get back to me. I decided to start limping back up the dirt road we had just come down. A few paces later, I sat down, crying. Elvis nudged my shoulder, and then whinnied to the departing mare and rider.

Groaning, I got up to move again, leading Elvis behind me. Every few steps, I'd have to stop. Elvis would take the tip of his nose and nudge me gently right under my rear end. At first I thought he was trying to wipe the blood off his face. But every time I would stop, he would give a nudge, lifting me slightly. I had seen this done with newborn foals, the mothers gently nudging them to help them to their feet and keep them moving.

Marilyn did make it down, and at the hospital, I learned I had bruised my thigh bone. When I treated Elvis's scrape, he snuffled my face and I received several horsey hugs. During my recuperation, a young teenager in the neighborhood offered to exercise Elvis around the subdivision we lived in. I agreed.

As I watched the young man heave up the saddle, Elvis stepped away from it. He tried tossing it again onto Elvis's back, and he pinned his ears, swished his tail and stepped away.

"Knock it off, Elvis," I growled. He nickered to me. Then the heavens opened, a light shone down, and I could hear a choir singing the Hallelujah chorus as I finally got it. Well, not the first part, but Elvis was grateful for the last part.

I understood now: Elvis had picked his rider.

THE HEART OF ELVIS

working with Elvis's travel companion, another young palomino-colored Fox Trotter. Mellow Yellow was his name, bestowed upon him by my proud husband, who had the honor of choosing him.

That evening, I gratefully enjoyed my husband's need for higher standards--the heat provided by the motorhome's furnace thawed my cold fingers while I cleaned and arranged tack for the third time. Recently, I had changed bits for Elvis to what is called a Mullen mouthpiece. It was a solid bar that arched just slightly, attached to a side shank that would give a little leverage if I needed it. It was considered a mild bit, and Elvis seemed to like it best. At the last second, I decided it needed to go with the black-leather bridle since that would stand out better against Elvis's graying color.

Sleep wouldn't come as, in my mind, I went over the trail course again and again. I was worried about the side passing and backing around the cones. I had practiced side passing over the logs in the parking lot, and it had not gone well. Elvis had tossed his head, pulling on the bit, dancing under me. I finally dismounted. From the ground, where we had our best communication, I patiently showed him what I wanted. With the log under him, he would have to cross both his front feet and back feet to move in a sideways motion. The hardest part of this maneuver was keeping his body straight so his front feet didn't get ahead of his back. If this happened he would be at an angle and more apt to step on the log, causing us to lose a point.

The next day, bedecked in cowgirl duds, a style

I disliked, I saddled a shiny Elvis with help from my husband. I was irritated at the new bridle as I struggled to get the bit in Elvis's mouth. He chewed and tossed his head, suddenly getting antsy. They called the Trail Class, and the moment was at hand. I swung up into the saddle and worked the reins lightly. Elvis ducked his head, chomping on the bit.

"Darrell, did you mess with his bridle this morning? It doesn't fit right," I grumbled, after jumping back down to check it.

Rolling his eyes, he snorted. "I don't touch your tack. I know nothing about it. You were the one working on it last night."

I shrugged it off, attributing it to my nerves being communicated to Elvis. Finally, it was my turn. My body tightened. We struggled a little with opening the gate, but as my heart slowed from ricocheting around my ribcage, I took a deep breath and remembered Charlie's advice: let Elvis do his job. Without hesitation, he went over the bridge, pivoted in the box easily and went off into his showy fox-trot, navigating the poles well. At the side pass, I settled deeper into the seat of the saddle and worked at giving direct leg pressure while balancing his head with the reins. He nicked the log with his hooves several times-- we were not straight--but he did his best at understanding. We got over the log.

The dreaded backup came, and I noticed he fidgeted as I pulled back gently on the reins, which put pressure on his tongue from the bit. Tossing his head and flipping his nose to get release from the bit, we weaved drunkenly around two of the cones, and I quit the fight for a backup, figuring at this point we had lost already with our clumsy side pass and inept backup attempt. We ended with a flourish at the mailbox. I opened the door, showed the mail, put it back in, showing I could indeed pick up my mail from horseback, and then he happily trotted to the gate. I headed back to the stall, mortified. It was nothing like the graceful dance I had hoped for. As I stripped off his bridle, I noticed the Mullen bit.

In my nervousness the night before, I had put the bit on the bridle upside down! This meant the slight arch that was supposed to push into the roof of his mouth had instead applied pressure to his tongue. Every time I had pulled on the bit, it had been more pressure than he'd ever had in his mouth before. I cried, hugging his neck. How had this gentle creature ever got stuck with such an imbecile partner?

"Robynn, hurry! They want you back in the ring," Dan, our friend, hollered at us as he came towards the stalls. His wife, Marilyn, was competing as well, and he'd heard my name being called. I had no time to tack back up, not knowing I was supposed to hang around until the end of the class.

I felt foolish running into the ring to stand next to the other mounted competitors. I wondered what they wanted. Only the winners should be in there, right? I got the second shock of the day: Elvis had won third place in Trail.

THE HEART OF ELVIS

Chapter Nine – The Rescue

In the spring of 2004, Elvis and I were very busy. I had "show" fever. We practiced every day. I reasoned that if we could win third place with an upside-down bit, imagine what we could do when it was right-side up! I also had a chronic back problem that was about to rearrange my life.

Through the years, there were times when the back spasms would be excruciating, but I would work, ride and push through them. Then one morning in May, I could not get out of bed. For the first time in my life, I spent the whole day in bed. Crawling out of bed the next morning, I felt a little better. Ibuprofen became my best friend, and like a squirrel, I stashed it everywhere.

I soldiered through the June shows. Elvis placed consistently in the top five, anywhere between third and fifth. My dream of first place in Trail continued to elude me. In July, I helped put up hay for the winter, bucking eighty-pound bales, until my back once again threw a fit. A few days later I was asked if I would help on a small cow roundup. Elvis was what we called an easy keeper. Meaning he just looks at hay and gains weight, which can cause many health issues in a horse. He needed the work.

Darrell saddled Elvis for me before I left, worry in his eyes. "Are you sure you're up for this?"

"Yes. I will just work it out through riding," I said, reassuring him.

I drove the pickup and trailer into my friend's barnyard, slowly getting out and taking Elvis out of the trailer. I checked in the saddlebags to make sure I had my stash of Ibuprofen, and worried that I might not have enough for the four– to six-hour cattle drive ahead of me.

There were five of us riding, and the horses were frisky with the cool morning air. As we trotted through a grassy valley, Elvis stumbled into a hole, jarring me. The most awful pain I'd ever had ripped down from my hip to my toes. Childbirth didn't even come close to it. I bent over the horn, gasping and waiting for the spasm to pass.

I searched in the saddlebag for another pill. Gritting my teeth, I continued following the group in front of me. We went up the side of a hill and stopped as Dave gave directions.

"We're going to split into two groups. I need three of you to ride up that ridge over there. Several pairs have been spotted in the pine and we need to push them back down to the gate we just came through. Two of us will ride up through the canyon and see if we can spot any more there."

He paired me with the other two ridge riders, and I knew immediately there was no way I could take the stress of the climb or coming back down. I felt terrible. I knew he needed the help. Three on a ridge were barely enough, but the pain was not easing; my toes were now numb. Anyone who has had nerve pain knows its mighty power.

"Dave, I just can't do it. I should have never come. My back is out and I have to go back. I'm so sorry."

What could he say? He nodded his understanding and asked if I could find my way back. At this point, there was no way I was going to tell him my secret. In the city, I go by landmarks. I can always find my way back from where I've been. Yet, in the hills and trees, it all looks the same to me--a frightening feeling when most of the time, I'm competent in finding my way around. I wasn't sure how to get back to the ranch.

My guilt kept me silent, and I waved them off as I turned Elvis around. At first, he balked. He didn't like leaving the "herd." Then, as we headed out, the pain became unbelievably worse. I no longer cared about where we were. Hunching over the saddle horn, trying to release pressure off the nerve that was raking agony down my leg, I knew if I got off, I would never be able to get back on. At this point I wasn't sure I could even walk.

Somewhere in those first few minutes, Elvis realized he was in charge. Sensing I had checked out, he began to pick his way back down the hill. When we got to the gate, those hours of practicing for the show paid off. I was able to open--with his help--and close the gate without dismounting. I looked like a wounded cowboy in a Western: barely hanging on to my trusty steed as he carefully stepped out, somehow knowing where the truck and trailer were.

The ride that had only taken a half hour out became an hour-and-fifteen-minute ride back. I sobbed quietly in pain, the reins loose as I depended on that gentle steed. At one point we had to cross a small bridge over a stream. A bevy of quail flew up out of the reeds, and Elvis froze in place, shuddering to keep from jumping sideways in surprise.

I never will know how he found that trailer. In the wide expanses of Wyoming, cell service is spotty at best. This day I was blessed to have a strong signal as I called my husband to come get me. There was no way I could drive.

The pain was relentless. I slid off, going into a crouch, still trying to get relief, holding onto the stirrup for balance. Elvis kept dipping his head to snuffle at my face, standing steady as I used the stirrup fender to pull myself up every now and then to try and release the spasm.

Once again, when we got home, Elvis was in

heaven with the treats showered on him.

Then, bad news from the doctor: my riding days could be over. I needed back surgery immediately.

THE HEART OF ELVIS

Chapter Ten – Getting Back in the Saddle

The wind howled outside of the arena. Inside, the riders were bundled against the frigid cold of a Wyoming February. The horses' coats were shaggy, and horse and rider's breath mingled in the air. I watched from the sidelines, my feet numb with cold.

The scar on my back was healing, but my mind still bore the fear of excruciating nerve pain. The doctor had reassured me that I had healed exceptionally well. I could go back to riding at any time. But there were those memories of pain only controlled by medication.

Elvis passed by, his shoulders rippling as he threw his front feet out, reaching. His long, luxurious tail hiked up in a rooster plume as his back feet landed a few inches ahead of where his front feet had just been. His head shook in rhythm with his every stride, his neck swelling in a beautiful arch. I could spend all day watching him move. He was horse-poetry in motion.

My granddaughter's face sported a smile that glowed with happiness. For several years, Jaquelynn had traveled with me to shows. She'd even participated several times in Model Class with Elvis, though he didn't stand a chance for placing because of his stocky build. But she had not ridden due to being so young and Elvis having so much fire. Jaquelynn had begged me to ride and I finally relented. I knew I had infected her with the dreaded "horse crazy" gene.

So once again, Elvis was being duded out. He seemed happy with the little girl perched on his back, but right now, he was up to his old tricks.

"Grandma, he won't quit heading for the gate."

Sure enough, every time he came around the arena, he would lean over towards the gate, and this time, he had stopped at it. This was his signal that the horsey ride was over.

"Honey, what is Elvis's first rule?"

A big sigh brought her shoulders into a droop.

She recited in a monotone, "If you don't tell him what you want, he doesn't have to do it. But Grandma, I'm trying; he's not listening."

My heart went out to her. I knew the frustration of not being able to speak horse. I was still learning myself. I instructed her once again on how to hold up the outside rein, to push, and kick with the outside leg as she and the horse came towards the gate. Two more passes proved to be her undoing. With tears in her eyes, she conceded defeat.

I struggled within myself. I knew what he needed: some re-direction and someone who could speak his language. And I knew I was the only one who could do it. But I was fearful that the doctor was wrong, and if Elvis tripped or fell, I would be back in the hospital again. I didn't want to get on him. For the first time in my life, I had no desire to ride.

Jaquelynn dismounted, her big brown eyes filled with disappointment. Her posture screamed dejection. Elvis nosed her, looking for an undeserved goody. Call it grandmotherly love--call it whatever you like--but I couldn't take it anymore.

Taking a big breath, I called out, "Bring him over to the fence. I will mount from there."

Jaquelynn's eyes opened wide. "Are you sure, Grandma? Will your back be okay?"

To ease her fears (and my own), I said, "It's okay. Elvis will take care of me."

I fervently hoped he didn't have a case of spring fever coming on and was about to make a liar out of me. I eased into the saddle, sitting for a moment to let my stiff back muscles relax into the saddle seat. Elvis turned his head, pricked his ears forward and sniffed my shoe. Turning back, he slowly moved off, walking carefully. Halfway around the arena, I applied leg pressure to his side and he transitioned smoothly into a faster walk. When I asked for the flatfoot walk, he didn't respond. I nudged his side with the heel of my foot again; he snorted, ducked his head behind the bit and purposely ignored my request.

At this point, I was irritated, but a little voice inside my head reasoned it out. A horse can feel a fly land on his skin and will ripple the skin to rid himself of the pest. They communicate within the herd with body language. Every ear twitch, tail swish, head swing and stomp of the foot meant something in their language. This was the first time since his summer rescue that I had gotten into the saddle. He could feel my stiffness and sensed I wasn't ready for anything jarring yet. I would just have to relax and trust him once again.

As we neared the gate, he dropped his shoulder, trying to angle towards the gate. "Knock it off, Elvis," I growled, applying my outside leg to his side, lifting the rein against his neck, warning him in horse language to keep from running through his shoulder. He flicked his ears back at me and obediently moved away.

As the summer approached, I began riding again but not near the level I had been doing the year before. By now, Jaquelynn and her younger sister, Katelynn, were both riding. Elvis was doing triple time between us.

I hired Jane as our instructor, and she became part of the family. She worked another Fox Trotter I had acquired by the name of Sherman. With her helping to lift saddles, I would be able to work into building up my back muscles. Her goal that summer was to get Sherman solid enough and quiet enough for me to ride. With my back problems, he was more spirited than I could handle at the time. We used the show to expose my horses to commotion. It helped create a sounder spirit within them.

At the first show that summer, I stood and watched as Jaquelynn and Elvis participated in their first Youth Trail Class. Elvis was giving her his best. Attentive to each of her cues, he moved quietly and methodically through bridge, side pass and into a flowing fox-trot. Tears clouded my vision as I watched them work together. When, at the end, she won first place, there was not a treasure in the world I valued more than her joy.

But I also didn't miss the irony of the moment either. The first-place ribbon in Trail, which I had coveted and tried so hard to accomplish, had just been won by my granddaughter!

THE HEART OF ELVIS

Chapter Eleven– The Heart of Elvis

I was standing next to Elvis, holding the reins, waiting for the next class. I did a lot of this during the show years. There was never a decent sound system in the arenas we competed in, so if you were anywhere but in the arena, you might miss a gate call and lose your chance at competing in the class.

Elvis tugged at the reins, trying to move away. In the crowded holding area, there were other riders either mounted or standing with their horses, waiting as I was. The Special Needs Class was competing, and added to the mix were family members watching the contestants by the arena rails. I kept a watchful eye out. It would be easy for someone to startle Elvis, and though he'd never done it, I feared he would kick or step on someone.

He tugged again at the reins, but I ignored him because I was talking with Jaquelynn.

"Grandma, I think Elvis wants to visit that little girl," Jaquelynn said, interrupting me.

I turned around, and there stood a young woman with a toddler holding on to her leg and looking up at Elvis. The little girl obviously had special needs of her own and was shy on top of that.

Elvis stretched his head down again towards the little girl, taking a step forward. I introduced myself to the mother. Elvis had a habit of showing interest in particular people. I was curious as to what had drawn his attention.

"My little girl is fascinated by your horse. The minute we came in, she started pointing at him. She doesn't talk but points at what she wants. We hope when she gets older, we can get her into Hoofbeats for Healing. I think the program would help her out, and she is crazy about horses."

As she talked, I loosened up on the reins, alternating between watching the little girl's face and Elvis's actions. Slowly, he put his head down to her level. She stepped back behind her mom but still peeked around her mother's leg. Elvis waited patiently, his ears pricked forward.

We continued to talk as the mother shared the little girl's issues. Elvis shook himself all over, and the little girl uttered a squeak and peeked at him from the other side of her mother. Elvis closed his eyes, head down, like he was out in pasture. Then the little girl sidled out to stand in front of her mom's legs, watching him intently. Slowly, she stepped forward and placed one little hand on his nose. His eyes opened but he stayed still. As if there was suddenly a magnetic pull, the little girl wrapped both arms around Elvis's nose and rested her little head on his forehead, gurgling and cooing. Elvis closed his eyes again, content to stay captured in her embrace. Before long, the little girl was sitting on his back, going between clapping and pitching forward to hug his neck. He had made another friend, something he seemed to enjoy doing.

I got used to being his manager, handler and agent. Elvis seemed to charm everyone. At one of the fairgrounds, I went into the arena during a lunch break to work with Elvis. As I got ready to mount up, a group of fairground workers came through. They were on a work-release program from the local jail--a mix of young people clad in bright-orange jumpsuits. Spying Elvis, they headed towards us. I was nervous as they approached, uncomfortable with what to say or do around jail inmates. The first thing they noticed was his unusual facial marking.

"Hey, lady, has he always had that half-and-half marking on his face? What's his name?" As they crowded around him, Elvis bowed his head, gently sniffing at each hand extended to him, nibbling here and there. I relaxed, watching Elvis make new friends. I noticed that for a moment, they were carefree little kids again, wanting a horse of their own. They petted and talked to him, remarking on his unusual name. When they departed, Elvis whinnied after them. I felt guilty that he had been so outgoing and trusting where I had been wary.

Many times I wondered, was it Elvis's nickname, his color or his character? Or maybe it was just an aura about him? I don't know exactly which one it was, but I do know Elvis was a people magnet. At a barbeque, I ran into the husband and wife who had owned Elvis's mother. They still remembered Elvis as a colt. They had seen his winnings at the MFTHB Show & Celebration listed in the MFT Journal and wanted to know how I had gotten him to work with me. They remembered his stubborn streak.

"Compromise and a lot of practice--trust me," I said. "But I've always wondered how he got his name."

"Well, my husband always named them after country-western singers, but I chose rock and roll. It was my turn, and as I was watching him run around the pasture, he had the most rocking and rolling gait I had ever seen. So I decided he was Elvis!"

I had to laugh. I knew just what she was talking about, having ridden him the first few years. She described his uneven gait perfectly. I also found out that Elvis's mother was blind in one eye. The gal said that mare was the most patient and kind mother, always careful not to step on her foals. I wondered if this was where Elvis had gotten his ability to sense in people their infirmities. I had done nothing to teach him this. It just seemed to be a natural talent of his.

There were so many little moments where his connection with people touched my heart. While traveling to or from a show, we would stop to let the horses out for food and water, and they would create a stir of picture taking and questions. I was moved to tears on a stop in Bozeman, Montana. We pulled into the local Walmart and parked over in the corner, close to the freeway on-ramp. We took the horses out, tied them to the trailer and offered them food and water.

A young man stumbled out of the bushes and trees lining the parking lot, making a beeline for Elvis. His clothes were rumpled; his face sported a couple days of stubble. As he approached, the fumes from his activities wafted ahead of him. I was startled by his intentness and nervous because he appeared homeless.

Elvis's response surprised me even more. Usually a little cautious, unless he was the one doing the seeking, he lowered his head to the stranger, nickering softly. The young man said nothing, acting like he didn't see me. Moving straight to the horse, he ran his hand down Elvis's shoulder while offering his other hand for Elvis to sniff. Then he wrapped his arms around Elvis's neck and sobbed quietly into the soft hair there. Elvis responded with his classic horse hug.

Frightened of this scruffy-looking man, I stood uncertain of what to do. My husband returned from buying a few quick groceries. He asked quietly, "What's going on?"

I shook my head in disbelief, whispering back,

"Really? I don't know. I don't know what to do with this guy."

Just as Darrell stepped forward to say something, the young man turned to us. "Sorry, folks. I just really miss them. I used to work with them all the time. I grew up on a ranch, and I've had some really fine horses. Things have just gotten really hard lately. I hope you don't mind. He's an awesome horse."

I gave the man a few horse treats and a water bucket to give Elvis, and we talked as he cared for the horse. He admitted to having an alcohol problem and wanting to get sober. He stroked Elvis's neck one more time, held Elvis's head with both hands and looked deeply into Elvis's eyes. He then thanked us for making his day, and turning abruptly, he disappeared into the bushes again. After he left my heart ached for him. I prayed his moment with Elvis gave him some peace and direction in his life.

I started to treasure these moments of "heart connections" that Elvis was prone to attract. I realized he managed to live up to his famous nickname. It also made me wonder about our connection. Had he sensed my brokenness in our first encounter? I chuckled at this thought. If he had, it had been a life-changing event for him! The thought also humbled me. We all carry pain, and he had the ability to soften it with his gregarious personality.

This side of him also made him a great show horse. I learned that his sensitivity to his rider's emotions, cues and directions created a picture of a willingness to perform. Even though he was willing, he also thought that gave him the right to be in charge. This was the basis for some of our difficulties in the show ring as well. Elvis could be quite a conundrum at times.

I continued to share him with everyone. Like all famous characters, he had admirers. His biggest fan became a little girl who thought she was afraid of horses at one time.

At every show, they need people to hand out ribbons, and the kids always offer to do it. For some reason, it seems like fun to them. During one show where I was busy going back and forth between riding two horses, my granddaughter Jaquelynn offered to hand out ribbons and was introduced to Maddy. They were close in age and bonded immediately. Maddy had serious health problems, but it didn't seem to affect her determination to have fun and enjoy life, except for riding horses. Her legs were frail, and the size of the creatures intimidated her.

Jaquelynn refused to accept this and brought Maddy over to meet Elvis. Within minutes, Elvis had worked his magic. Bending his head graciously, eating treats gently from her hand, Maddy gave him kisses on his soft nose. I watched as Jaquelynn and Maddy wandered around the holding area that evening (after the classes) with Elvis following them docilely, like an oversized puppy.

Maddy asked if she could have a ride on Elvis. I told her if it was okay with her father, it was fine with me. He was more than willing and helped get her up on Elvis. With Jaquelynn on one side and Maddy's father on the other, Elvis carefully carried his biggest fan. The energy from her smile could have lit a city.

Even to this day, to my joy, when Jaquelynn and Maddy get together, her first question is always, "How's Elvis?"

Chapter Twelve – Elvis the Character

For every action, there is an equal and opposite reaction. Everything has a balance, and Elvis was no different. For all of his good, wonderful traits, he could also be quite a handful, and those who underestimated Elvis learned firsthand a lesson in humility. At a show in Powell, I ran into Tony and Cindy, Elvis's first owners. They had seen an article about Elvis in the MFTHBA Journal. I know I had a mischievous grin while listening to Tony complain. "That dang horse made quite a liar out of me, didn't he? Who'd have believed that Elvis-the-ugly-duckling would turn into Elvis-the-show-horse?"

I didn't find Elvis's aptitude for rising above

people's expectations as humorous when it involved me. Early in his life, Elvis suffered a hock injury. The vet warned me he'd never be a barrel-racing horse but with careful riding and consideration, he should live to a ripe old age. Unfortunately, one of the classes needed for a Versatility title was Barrels. I never pushed him around the barrels, and coming back to the gate after the pattern was what Elvis liked best. The only challenge I had was stopping him before we got to the gate! Our times were always the longest. I would tell people it was okay when we lost because someone had to be last and that was our job.

I remember Jaquelynn asking me one summer, "Grandma, can I ride Elvis in the Barrels Class? I think he can go faster and do better times."

I laughed. "Honey, he can't go any faster. He's just too fat and not cut out to be a barrel racer."

Like others in the past, I doubted Elvis's abilities. Jaquelynn set her jaw, a determined light in her eyes, and off to practicing she went.

I watched through the dust and dirt that arose from their practice efforts tearing around the barrels. Jaquelynn taught Elvis to find the pocket, that perfect spot where he could turn and save the most time going around the barrel. She worked with his habit of taking the right lead and his desire to race back to the gate.

At the end of that summer, a large manila envelope arrived from the MFTHBA office. It held the results of the summer show season. I opened it eagerly, and to my chagrin read that Elvis and Jaquelynn were the National Youth High Point winners in Barrels in

2009. Just as in 2008, they had done the same, of course, in Trail.

Even though he had a dominant personality, Elvis and I had a pact. He was number one in the pasture, the king of his world, until the saddle was on. Then, leadership was supposed to transfer to me, the rider. With an uneducated rider or child, it became a whole different game. Elvis quickly sized up his rider and went to their level, giving only what he thought he had to give.

I was blessed with several grandkids who wanted to ride and show. Katelynn was talented but not as driven to achieve as Jaquelynn. While on a two-week show circuit, I kept asking her, "Do you think you might want to practice with Elvis for your class tomorrow?"

She'd shake her head and answer lightly, "No, he will do it." I knew that most of the time, Elvis did. Until he finally decided he was in charge.

Jane and I discussed Katelynn's lack of interest several times and decided not to nag her. Instead I would let it play out and see what Elvis would do. At the Davis County Fairgrounds in Utah, I stood at the rail watching Katelynn go into the next class to compete. Jaquelynn had just ridden him in the previous class and done quite well. But with Katelynn now in the saddle, Elvis sensed there was no direction, and he decided he was going to do what he wanted. Katelynn was not prepared. I could see that she was struggling to communicate with him. Coming around the ring for the third time, she called to me.

"Grandma, he won't do what I'm asking." I bit my lip. The desire to see the grandkids do well and feel the pride of accomplishment was the whole reason I let them ride. It was tough letting her learn the hard way.

"Just do your best, Katelynn. You have to make him listen to you," I called back.

Elvis learned that he got to rest in the middle of the arena when the class was over and the judges did their final inspection. He liked to interact with the judges during that time. This show had three judges standing in the middle of the ring, making note of the contestants and their performances. I observed him veer off from the arena wall and casually walk over to the first judge, nudging his clipboard, almost like he was saying, "Hi. Whacha doin?" The judge looked down, his face working to keep a serious demeanor. Jane and I couldn't contain our mirth.

Katelynn was red-faced and flustered. Normally, she had a passive personality, but Elvis was pushing her buttons. She pulled on the reins, trying to redirect him back to the arena wall. Instead, Elvis walked in a wide arc and went to the next judge, who had to turn away from him, tears springing up in her eyes as she held back her laughter. I was torn between giggling and feeling sorry for my granddaughter. Finally, Katelynn got mad, and I could tell she suddenly remembered Elvis's first rule. If you didn't give him the right cues, he didn't have to do it. With a firm hand on the reins and her little legs thumping to get his attention, she got Elvis back to the wall.

I watched her little lips press together; her

80

brows lowered and her back stiffened. Elvis suddenly became a beautiful picture of motion, obediently following her cues. I smiled to myself. It was a tough lesson, but I was proud that she hadn't given up.

There were five kids in the class. Jane and I expected her to place last. Instead, she placed third. Once Elvis started fox-trotting correctly, he was hard to beat. Her face was lit up with a relieved smile as she rode out of the arena clutching her yellow ribbon. "Grandma, I'm going to ride Elvis tonight. We need to practice. He's not doing that again!" I just grinned, nodding my head in a sage manner. Later, the judges shared with me that it had been very hard not to laugh when he came to visit. Elvis just had a way of sucking up to the judges.

I found, when I had ridden him, there were times in the ring that he could be fiercely competitive, his gait right on, and eager to perform. Other times, he'd lag down, taking his time, trying to duck out gates, and was slow or overreacted to cues. In defense of Elvis, sometimes the rider was the problem. But just like us, animals have their good and bad days.

My grandson Derick, only twelve days younger than Jaquelynn, was even more horse crazy than most but had a deadly allergy to horse dander. I was very proud of him when he decided to go through several years of allergy shots to achieve his dream of riding. Elvis took to teaching him rule number one immediately, which was if the right language wasn't spoken, Elvis didn't have to do what was asked.

I noticed Derick was naturally talented in

sitting astride a horse. Unfortunately he offset that talent with hands that couldn't always feel the tension needed on the reins. Of all the kids who'd ever ridden him, I observed that Elvis seemed to take exception to Derick, not treating him with his usual patience. To make it worse, Derick, unlike Jaquelynn, hadn't had the time to practice and get to know Elvis. He had to work hard to catch up.

Recovering from my second back surgery, I assembled a team of grandkids one summer to do the show circuit. They were a great combination of personalities and got along fairly well. All were driven in their desire to learn and ride.

I gave each one a job. Derick was in charge of Elvis's care. Jaquelynn had moved on to a little Fox Trotter mare called Sequoia, and Trent would be the gopher, as I was still under doctors' restrictions. All the kids (myself included) hated to take care of Elvis since he seemed to have pig genes when it came to keeping his stall and himself clean. Being mostly white with black points, he delighted in sleeping in his poop, leaving dark stains that had to be scrubbed right before you had to show him. I never saw a horse who could mash poop so finely into pine shavings, making cleaning out his stall with the muck rake a nightmare.

It irritated me that Elvis seemed to go out of his way to get dirty for Derick, even getting it on his face and working it into his mane, despite our best efforts to keep him clean. While I was helping Derick to bathe Elvis at the wash rack, I had to duck as Elvis swatted at Derick with his soapy tail. He didn't seem to appreciate Derick's efforts to help him with his horsey hygiene.

"Knock it off Elvis," I snarled. Elvis laid back his ears and stepped towards Derick, swinging his haunches into him. I immediately went to his hip, tapping it in warning to get him to move away from Derick. It was apparent to me Elvis did not respect him. Yet, Derick worked hard to make sure Elvis was well cared for.

In the middle of the season, while we waited for a class to be called, I glanced over at Derick as he stood holding Elvis's reins. He looked quite the cowboy in his white shirt, black hat and jeans. Needing water, he handed the reins off to Trent, who'd also been working with Elvis. As he stood a little behind Elvis's hip, drinking a bottle of water and chatting with Jaquelynn, Elvis's tail lifted slightly. I assumed Elvis was letting off gas until I watched him step closer to Derick and let out a steaming mound of excrement. It bounced off Derick's sleeve, landing with a warm plop on his boots.

I knew then, that just like people, some personalities don't mix. I had Derick change horses. He was given Mellow, a lovely palomino-colored Fox Trotter I had been riding until my back surgery. I was delighted when they bonded, and Derick improved significantly as a rider.

That left Trent to work with Elvis. By the middle of the summer, I was given a doctor's release and decided the only horse that I could ride was Elvis. So Trent and I agreed to share him. Besides, I had to ride Elvis every now and then to remind him of the cues he was supposed to be responding to.

I had to smile as he sat in the saddle. Trent's short legs barely made it to the stirrup. His look of determination as he flapped them against Elvis's side would have been amusing, if it hadn't been so frustrating for Trent. Elvis was a little kinder with him, but Trent still had to work hard to communicate with him.

In Showmanship, you are judged on how well you can work a pattern with your horse from the ground with just a halter on the horse's head and a lead line attached to it. It was one of my favorite classes, and Elvis was very responsive to it. Patiently, I worked with Trent as I had with the grandkids before him. I watched, calling out directions and suggestions as Trent tugged Elvis into a walk or a trot in our graveled driveway between the cones I set out. "Give him slack on the lead rope right before you bring up your energy to take off. He will sense it and move out with you," I patiently instructed.

At the next show, I had just finished competing in Amateur Showmanship when I handed Elvis off to Trent for Beginner Youth Showmanship. He had paid extra attention to his outfit, looking dapper in a tightly tucked plaid shirt, black jeans and cowboy hat. He waited stiffly during the long show classes that performed before his turn.

Finally, it was time for him to line up. I noted that Elvis patiently waited by his side with a foot cocked, dozing. The three judges at the end of the arena motioned for Trent to start the Showmanship pattern. He stepped up with a tug on the lead rope. Elvis moved his front two feet, stopped, extended his back feet and let it all hang out to pee. I put my hand over my mouth to stifle my laughter. Trent came up short on the lead line, looking back at Elvis in panic. Then he turned to look at me, mortified, frozen, and not knowing what to do.

I quickly regained my composure and called from the railing, "Honey, just let him finish!" The judges at the end of the course covered their faces with their clipboards as they laughed. The announcer saw Trent's dilemma and stepped up to help him.

"Well, folks, we are going to have a short break here. Then we will start the pattern over." To add to all of our uncontrollable laughter, Elvis now let out a long moan as he finished the job. The announcer again covered.

"Well, folks, when you got to go, you got to go!"

Trent, a deep shade of red, patiently waited. When Elvis was done, he raised his chin like a true showman and started the pattern again. Biting my lip, I watched as they walked, turned, backed up and pivoted together in sync. I hugged him tight when he won first place. The crowd's applause had a ring of true appreciation for a job well done.

Often these little instances reminded me that no matter how frustrating he could be at times, Elvis was quite the character.

THE HEART OF ELVIS

Chapter Thirteen – The First Blue Ribbon

I will never forget--because I pouted about it--where and when Elvis and I won our first blue ribbon. We won it in the Western Pleasure Class in Colorado, and this foreshadowed the future. Jane and Darrell were shocked by my childish attitude, but I didn't care. It simply was not the ribbon I wanted.

Elvis and I had practiced almost to the point of death. The patterns were getting more difficult as time went on and the contestants got better. They had started adding canters to the Amateur Division patterns. We'd both eaten our weight in arena dust learning how to canter on cue. Even though I had just done the perfect pattern in Trail, we'd placed third against another horse that had balked at every obstacle.

Let me explain. A Trail course is made up of different obstacles that a horse and rider have to negotiate well. Points are given for each obstacle. The more smoothly and quietly your horse negotiates these obstacles, the better you score in points. You have to follow the pattern exactly. No deviations. If you go off pattern, you are disqualified. So if you had to side pass your horse over a log to the right but instead you did it to the left, you would be disqualified. If you missed an obstacle, you would be disqualified. And so on.

As we entered the arena, my heart soared with pride as he picked up a canter immediately, which was usually a struggle for us. Slowing down, I worried he would balk at working to open a rope gate, something we had never done. Considering that the rope was white and looked like the electric fence I used during the summer in the horse pasture, he responded to my cues with a level head. We side passed up to the rope. I lifted it off the post, shifting my weight back, pulling on the reins slightly. Cautiously, he backed up. Softly, I pressured with my outside leg, and he carefully pivoted, bringing his front end through, stepping through; then, responding to my continued cues, he now swung his backend through, backed up and I was able to put the rope back on the pole. I took a big breath. I'd been holding it during the procedure. We continued through the next obstacles, relaxed and confident.

Excitement built as I sat waiting at the end of the class with the other competitors. I glanced up and down the line. I figured I had a pretty good chance. Only one other horse-rider team had come close to our run. When the places were called, I was shocked. I hadn't won my longed-for blue ribbon in Trail. I rode out, patting Elvis, telling him it didn't matter. He had done well.

Anger began to mount as I pulled the saddle off Elvis. I complained bitterly to Jane as she filled Elvis's water bucket in his stall. "That buckskin and his rider shouldn't have placed over us. The horse bucked when it started a canter, shied, boogied and balked at every obstacle." Jane quietly informed me that I didn't even deserve that. I, who had bragged about having a photographic memory, had gone off pattern.

No way! I thought. I couldn't have gone off pattern. Jane didn't know me well enough to know about my infamous temper. Darrell just disappeared. He had felt the lash of my displeasure more than once and knew better than to hang around. I guess he felt it was every man for himself and left Jane to figure it out. I took a deep breath, holding back my anger as I argued with her.

"I beg to differ, Jane. I did that pattern spot-on."

Again, she quietly repeated, "No, you did not. You went the opposite way around the barrels. You were supposed to take the figure eight to the left of the barrel, not the right."

I threw back that Elvis was not a left-leaded

horse. Just as every human can be either left– or right-handed, horses are the same. When they pick up to lead off in a canter, they can favor either their left or right front leg. Elvis liked to pick up a lead with his right front leg.

I continued to argue, refusing to budge. "It doesn't matter which way; it was still a figure eight. Besides, that other lady's horse was scared of the whole course. There is no way they should have placed over us."

Jane shook her head, stubbornness settling in along the muscles in her jawline. "No, you have to do it the right way. The only reason you took third is because you and Elvis were smooth and right on everything else. By rights, you shouldn't have even placed because there were six horses in that class."

Again, in the rules, if you disqualify (or DQ), you cannot place above another horse that didn't. That meant the three horses behind me had also gone off pattern. At that point the judge simply had to rate the best of the worse. At least I had that as a consolation, right? Nope. At this point I just began a pity party with a Godzilla attitude to go with it.

I left Darrell and Jane to discuss my childish temper and sought out the only being in the world who understood my frustration. Elvis stood quietly in his stall as I hugged his neck, wetting his silken hair with my bitter tears of disappointment. So you can understand why later, when Elvis and I won our first blue ribbon ever, I was bitter. No?

In Western Pleasure, the goal is to walk, fox-trot, stop and canter on cue from the announcer. You must have good equitation (sitting straight, heels down, looking like you are glued to the saddle). The horse-rider team must create a picture of a pleasant ride with smooth transition in gait changes. Elvis was a looker. His gray color,--with black-pointed markings--flowing, white tail and regal carriage always made a beautiful picture. He'd caught the eye of this particular judge more than once.

I was still upset. My mind wasn't even in the competition. I was relaxed, and Elvis did what he did best: show off. We went into the ring, transitioning smoothly into the gaits that were called for. As the results went to the announcer, I leaned over and patted Elvis's neck, thinking about cancelling our last class. When they called my name for first place, ungratefully, with a stiff smile, I received the ribbon.

I stood waiting, holding Elvis's reins, watching as the next class went around the arena, showing off their skills to the judge. I noticed Dallin, a young man that had been cheated by nature with twisted limbs who didn't let it slow him down. He had a heart-desire to ride. As they called the winners, I heard a cheer go up for him. Riding out of the arena, there had never been a grander smile. His thin arm held high the pink ribbon designating his fifth-place winning. I watched as he was helped off his horse, still chattering excitedly about his win.

Hindsight is twenty/twenty, and I seemed to be very nearsighted. Jane had been right: I'd gone off pattern. I repented of my foolish ways and poor sportsmanship. Our first-place ribbon in Western Pleasure signaled a shift in our communication. I didn't recognize the gift at the time. In the show season before this one, Elvis and I had always placed towards the bottom. From this point on, Elvis would now place more often in the top three.

My ungrateful heart was melted by Dallin's infectious joy. Here was a young man who had overcome so much, showing such excitement over a last-place winning. I remembered how I used to find happiness in just getting a ribbon as well.

Chapter Fourteen – The Big Time

I had my sights set on going to Ava, Missouri for the MFTHBA's 2007 Fall Show and Celebration.

This was the biggest show of the year, the great one, where if you even got a ribbon, you counted yourself lucky. In the Fox Trotter world, this was where it had all began. I felt it was time for Elvis to show them what he could do.

Except that now, while performing in Trail Class, I had my doubts as the sweat trickled down my back. Two days of performing in high heat in a humid arena seemed to be sapping all of our energy, creating a meltdown. I concentrated, my body tense, asking Elvis with my leg for a canter. I felt him bunch under me, throwing his front feet out in an uneven cadence. Quickly I shortened the reins, tucking his nose, and asking again with my leg. Too late, we were at the side-pass obstacle. Lining him up next to the logs, I again cued with my leg. He wouldn't straighten, knocking the wooden poles out of alignment with his feet. I took a big breath. "Relax!" I told myself. Now asking for a fox-trot, I felt Elvis pull on the reins, trying to take a canter. Frustrated, I growled under my breath, "Knock it off, Elvis!"

Trail Class was a disaster. We rearranged every obstacle in the course. Jane stood at the arena entrance, watching. She was working with Sherman, another one of my Fox Trotters who needed experience. Shaking her head as I left the arena, she asked, "Why are you pushing so hard?"

"It's not me, Jane. It's him. I don't know what's wrong. Maybe it's the heat," I threw back irritably.

"I have to warn you," she said. "The heat and humidity are going to be even worse in Ava." I felt a childish urge to stick my tongue out at her.

Reining was up next. This was our worst class. I decided if he wouldn't pick up a canter heading towards the gate (he loved to run to it), then we were done. I would pull him from any further classes.

The judge looked shocked when I requested to leave in the middle of the Reining pattern. After the show, he asked why we had quit. He told me he'd seen much worse performances. I couldn't help thinking that if we had continued, he would have changed his mind about that.

Frustration hammered against my dreams and efforts. After each show, I debated with myself, trying to decide if we were ready. The Show & Celebration was a seven-day event versus the three-day event we were used to. I knew we might not be able to hold up under the stress, and there was the worry about Elvis's old hock injury. The Montana show marked the middle of the summer. I had expected to have made my decision by then. But it looked very doubtful that we could pull off Ava.

I went home discouraged. We practiced more. Then, at the last show of the season, we rallied. Having placed first in most of the classes we competed in, except, of course, the elusive first place in the Trail Class, Ava looked to be within our reach.

"Grrr, Elvis! Why is it you can do patterns perfectly at home and not at the show?" I growled during a training session. My granddaughter, waiting her turn to ride him, piped up, "It's because you are nervous, Grandma." Jane shrugged, trying to hold back the enigmatic smile on her face.

I rolled my eyes at them, but I had to admit that, in all fairness to Elvis, it wasn't his fault. I could just imagine his frustration at repeatedly crossing bridges and opening gates that lead to nowhere. Or Jane, who would watch us perform and think we were going to make it until my nerves kicked in. Then she'd wonder what the heck I was doing when I would go off pattern.

I held on to my dream despite all of the setbacks. Sitting down at the kitchen table, I figured up the budget and sat back staring at the numbers. The little kid in me finally won out. I had to try. I finally decided this was the year for the Show & Celebration. My husband bought me a tent camper for the back of the truck. I asked Jane to go with me. Darrell refused to camp out for two weeks in dry camping conditions--with no electricity or TV--and just horses going around in circles to look at.

Even though Jane, in the past, had met up with me at shows, this would be our first road trip together, and I was a little nervous. I have idiosyncrasies that I was afraid would ruin our friendship . . . such as my penchant to live on fast food and chocolate while she was into healthy eating. There were also my attention-deficit tendencies, my infamous temper and my perfectionist issues. Living in the tight quarters of a tent camper was sure to bring all these issues into clear focus.

Two weeks before the trip, after a huge amount of preparation, Elvis threw a shoe and came up lame. I was frantic. At first the vet said no to the trip, but after a week of Elvis standing in sand to allow the hoof wall to mend, I got two more opinions and it was a go.

I could write a book on just that one trip! I would title it Two Westerners go East. Most of the stories created on that trip were not about Elvis though, so I will save that for another time.

Loaded up with two horses, hay for two weeks and everything I thought we'd possibly need, we headed out. This would be a two-day trip and over 1,200 miles. We got into a good pattern-- letting the horses out at every gas fill-up--and made it to York,

Nebraska, in the evening just as a huge downpour hit. Of course, our raincoats were in the tack room of the horse trailer, and the tent camper had to be put up. Thank heavens our host had a barn we could park in.

The next day, after a beautiful drive through Missouri's rolling hills capped with lush trees, we pulled into the Celebration showgrounds. I was surprised--and Elvis was delighted--to find that dry camping in Missouri was different than in Wyoming. Instead of a dry, dusty area with maybe a few sagebrushes, we were in a lush, grass-filled hollow surrounded by trees. We had a hill that was a straight up climb to get to the performing areas, but overall, it was heavenly. I was blissfully unaware of the fact that Missouri grows bugs ten times bigger than Wyoming, or I might not have viewed it as so pastoral.

In the coolness of the next afternoon, I swung my leg over the saddle. Elvis was staring at the country road ahead of us, eager to move out. We had come down a few days before the show to help the horses acclimate to the humidity and heat. Practice was behind us. It was time to enjoy the countryside. Riding down the little, white dirt roads shaded by huge trees, I found myself immersed in the reason I owned horses. The clopping sound their feet made and the cool breeze on my face was the perfect combination for relaxation.

The next day I toured the MFTHBA office's museum and found a picture of Elvis's great-granddaddy, Zane Grey. I was amazed at how this stud had stamped his offspring. Elvis looked very similar to him in build and color. Except for that strange marking of a half-and-half colored face.

That evening I had my first chance to try out the oval track that was the front show ring. I felt a reverent awe as Elvis moved out with an even stride on the limestone track. The sun was setting, a welcomed coolness from the heat of the day settling in. Looking between Elvis's ears, I could see that the track ahead had been beaten down into the perfect surface for performance by years of competition. There was a feeling of connection to the history of the showgrounds as I realized Elvis and I rode together on the very track that his great-granddaddy, Zane Grey, had fox-trotted to victory on.

The Costume Class started off the show. Still in awe that I was actually going to compete in the Show & Celebration, I was nervous going into the show ring for the first time. I was proud of the little horse under me as he ignored my stiffness and swept around the track in his favorite gait, the cadence sounding smooth and correct. This was in spite of his flowing cape, and me, dressed as Elvis. I threw out T-shirts and posters with a classic picture of him on them. I was touched by the people who asked for one. I was never more surprised than when we placed fourth.

Earlier that day, I had told Jane that if Elvis won even one ribbon, then it was all worth it. We would have accomplished what I came for. Lying in the tent camper that night, I gazed up in amazement at the lone ribbon hanging on the support strut. It was outlined in the faint light coming from the grounds' light on top of the hill. In the darkness of the top bunk,

Jane stirred, her voice laced with a tremor of a chuckle. "Well, now that you have won the ribbon you came for, does that mean we can go home?"

THE HEART OF ELVIS

Chapter Fifteen
MFTHBA's 2007 Fall Show and Celebration

Jane had been right. It was ninety degrees and humidity had to be just as high. The Versatility Arena was uncovered, and the sun was showing no mercy. I wore a black hat and black show coat, which created my own personal sauna. Showmanship was a class I thought I had a slim chance of getting a ribbon in. Of course, it was also a dreaded pattern class.

I waited, holding the lead rope. Elvis stood

squarely, his gentle brown eyes watching as intently as mine for the judge's nod. With a tug on the lead rope, we started running through soft sand as he fox-trotted with me. Stopping beside me, in sync, he then pivoted perfectly. I remembered the "quarter method" of where I was supposed to be standing, as the judge walked around and viewed my horse. Certain we had nailed it and exhilarated it was done, I strode away from the judge to line up. Waiting for the other contestants to finish, I gave my best rodeo-queen smile while keeping Elvis standing square.

Relieved it was over, I watched the next competitor's performance, and suddenly, my stomach knotted. I had gone off pattern! I had been so focused on getting the pivot right that I had forgotten to ask him to back up four steps. As disappointment washed over me, I irritably wondered where all the darn flies were coming from . . . until I looked down and realized that, in the class before us, someone had left behind a smelly pile. Not only had I lined up with it unconsciously, but now we couldn't move away from it. Having been the first one out, we would have to stand there until eight more competitors ran through their patterns. Well, it was okay, I thought, because I felt just like that pile.

That evening, I would redeem myself, and Elvis would shine. The MFTHBA showgrounds were split. The front, oval, racetrack-like ring, was for Performance-based classes. The back arena was filled with dirt like a Western arena. The English Class would be held in the front ring. In a class of twenty-seven, I had no hope of a first place but thought maybe we could come in tenth. In the gleam of stadium lights, horses groomed to the max shone brightly, and any bling or metal twinkled. The coolness of the evening was also greatly appreciated.

As we went around the back side of the ring, I was feeling proud. Sitting there looking every bit the professional, Elvis responded smoothly to every cue. It was a perfect ride . . . until the bug hit me in the face.

My left eye reacted swiftly in defense, tightly capturing one of the bug's legs. There were five judges positioned strategically around the ring. They saw everything. In English, it is a no-no to let go of a rein and adjust anything. I panicked. The bug was squirming, wanting to be away from me as much as I wanted it gone. Yet, my eye, in reflex-defense mode, wouldn't open. Finally, down the backstretch, I passed a judge who was looking at the horse behind me, and with a quick swipe of my hand, the bug was gone-- along with any shred of pride I had left. Somehow, we placed sixth. I treasure that ribbon to this day.

As an out-of-state member, it's a big deal to receive a ribbon in the front ring. Jane and I marveled at how our little line of ribbons was growing. She was riding Sherman, again to help him gain confidence, and she was just as excited as I to get even a tenth-place ribbon.

During one ride in the front ring for a Performance Two-Gait Class, Elvis struggled as we came around the top of the track. The ring had a slight rise there, and as we rounded the corner, Elvis lost his rhythm. I wasn't sure if it was the rise or the attraction of the gate; either way, we would break our stride and struggle to come back into it.

All along the railing, trainers and owners were shouting instructions to their riders. Jane was off getting ready with Sherman. Suddenly, towards the end of the arena, where the crowd thinned out, a man standing by the rail spoke as I went around, "Tuck his nose."

I thought I was hearing things. Again, as I came around, I heard, "You're doing good; keep his shoulder up in the turn." This continued until our class was called. Elvis learned quickly that he got to rest on the grass oval in the middle of the track, which also became a new source of attraction. I had to be really focused on his movements or I would find us running over judges as he headed to the grass.

Afterwards, I looked for my encourager and finally found him in the practice ring.

I introduced myself, and he told me to call him Jim. "He's a Zane Grey, isn't he?"

"Why, yes, he is." I was amazed he picked up on Elvis's breeding. He then went on to talk about the different breed lines and the history of the Missouri Fox Trotter. I thanked him again for his help.

"You look scared out there. Don't be. That horse knows what to do. Just enjoy the ride."

I took his advice. In the Versatility Arena in the back, Elvis continued to win ribbons. Jane and I started to compete for the places we were missing. They judged from first through tenth. The eighth-place ribbon continued to elude us. It was a nice brown color. We had quite the rainbow in our tent camper now.

It had rained during the night, creating puddles throughout the Versatility Arena. The Trail-Class obstacles were set and ready to go. I waited my turn, my fingers playing nervously with the end of the Rommel reins. I stared at the rickety, small gate Elvis and I would have to maneuver through. This was it, the end of the long trail of training. Winning this class would be a fairy-tale ending.

Elvis moved his shoulder into the gate, trying to help me out. I had to ask him to back off. After a less-than-smooth start getting the gate open, we found our stride. But while backing up between two logs, Elvis decided he needed to take a load off his mind. I wasn't sure what to do as he paused to relieve himself. Then, he didn't want to step in it. He swung his back end, ticking rails with his hooves. Each tick cost us a point.

At the end, when the winners were announced, I struggled with my disappointment over the third-place ribbon. Tears threatened while I scrambled to remind myself it was an honor. I had been up against the best. We had not gone off pattern; I was at least proud of that.

Introducing myself to the first-place winner, I congratulated her. Excitement still danced in her eyes as she said, "Your horse is beautiful. I love grays. I thought you had us beat. I've been trying for this ribbon for over six years." Thanking her for her compliment, I learned she had overcome personal and physical issues to do it. At that point I knew it just wasn't our time yet.

With the Trail Class behind me, I could relax. It rained for a good portion of the show. Torrential downpours turned the track and the back arena into sloppy mud. Our last class in Versatility was Barrels. While rain pelted us, Elvis and I sloshed around the barrels, sending sprays of water everywhere. We might have gotten a better time if we had done a backstroke instead! I began to feel like we were doing more Celebration Aquatics than showing.

The last day, it had rained on and off for most of the day. The final World Grand Championship Performance classes would be held that evening. The staff worked tirelessly to get the small ponds created by the rainwater pumped off the track. Jane and I had finished all our classes, so we decided to watch the Championships.

The riders wore their best bling. Ladies' shirts sparkled, belts twinkled and each horse's hide had a high sheen under the lights. The best of the best came fox-trotting in, one after another, their heads shaking with colorful ribbons mixing into the flying manes. With a crack of thunder, the downpour began as they trotted around.

I had learned that the Missouri Fox Trotter had been bred to be a versatile horse. To pull the plows, move the timber, bring the carriages to town, be sure-footed in the mountains and still be a comfortable ride for the owner. Besides all of that, they were bred to have a sound mind, a gentle nature and willingness to do anything put to them. I was watching that breeding prove itself as both riders and horses got soaked through. They continued to plow through the small lakes, water splashing and spraying everywhere. The horses didn't slow or miss a beat of the fox-trot. It was this spirit that made me love the breed so much. It was quite a sight!

I left Ava, Missouri with stars in my eyes. We had taken in over 30 ribbons between us. I had only hoped for one. I felt that for the first time in this journey, I was finally becoming a horseman, and Elvis was the greatest partner ever.

THE HEART OF ELVIS

Chapter Sixteen - The King and I

Elvis was king in his own pasture, except when I stepped into the situation. Then I was number one, though at times we had to negotiate an understanding on different things. By now, through all the showing, we had definitely overcome the language barrier. I had learned some "horse" and he had learned some "English," and we both continued to improve on our bilingual skills.

He was the head of my little herd of four horses. Through the years when I brought the colts in, he would allow them to eat with him, but he chased away the older horses. After about a year, he would run the grown colts off, and they were on their own. He was always fair-minded but greedy when it came to hay.

In the spring, when the tender green shoots popped up out in the pasture, he didn't like to come in when I called. All my horses learned that if they came when I whistled, there was always grain or a goody waiting for them. But to Elvis, fresh spring grass trumped that. When they all came in, the minute I picked up a halter, Elvis would nonchalantly wander out the gate, putting his rear end to me (a grave insult), ignoring my calls to come back.

So I would fire up the four-wheeler and go out into the pasture to get him. The object of this was to teach Elvis that it was much wiser and less work to come into the corrals than be chased all over by the faster four-wheeler. After about ten years of this routine, I'd had enough.

"Darrell, don't open the gate to the corrals until I say so," I warned him. All the horses had come in, and, as usual, Elvis had made a beeline for the pasture when he saw the halter. He trotted off ahead of me, kicking and bucking out at the four-wheeler on his heels. Then I ramped it up a bit, going faster, pushing him. He snorted and moved out ahead of me easily. This went on until he was galloping hard, not stopping to kick anymore.

He headed to the gate, stopped, confused. Normally after one run, he headed in like a good boy, and it was all over. Instead, this time, I pushed him out to pasture again. After several stops at the gate in hopes of getting in, I finally hollered for Darrell to open the gate. Elvis went in gratefully, and that was the last time he ever turned his butt to me and walked off.

Another rule we had to work out was not mobbing the person with the grain bucket. The most dangerous time in my herd was when I would go to feed grain. All of them were greedy for it. In the winter, sometimes it would drop as low as thirty-degrees below zero. I would offset the plain grass hay I fed with a little grain.

They would push and shove at the feeder, sometimes bumping me in the process. I had taken to carrying a stick to protect myself when I went in. I had been watching Elvis at the feeder. All he had to do was pin his ears back, threaten to kick out with a hind foot, and they all backed off from him. So, one afternoon I decided I would try this out. They didn't know how much strength was in my kick--only that I was head-mare to them.

So I went in with the grain bucket firmly in hand and no stick. They started crowding as I dumped it into the low feeder. I swung my head to one side, glaring at them. Then I swung my head to the other side, and they hesitated. It only lasted a few seconds before they started pressing in again. I kicked back behind me. They scattered, giving me plenty of room until I was done. With a smug smile, I went to the gate to leave, unimpeded by crowding horses.

When I came into the house, my husband was frowning with a perplexed look in his eyes.

"What the heck was that all about?"

Suddenly I felt quite silly. "What? I was just talking horse. Elvis does that and they leave him alone. I figured it would work for me," I said with a defensive tone.

He laughed, shaking his head.

During the show years, there were times when Elvis didn't seem to be in the mood to trot or canter in a class. I learned a trick to get him to work harder and be showier. You have to rate how fast your competitors are going. If they are going slower, you have to cut into the ring and pass them. You never want to overshadow another competitor for very long because this could block the judge from seeing them. I was always careful to find a horse that was slightly faster than Elvis. My friend, Thea, consistently competed in the same division and classes, so I would put him behind her stallion. Elvis was determined to pass that stallion, and chased him for years. This helped keep him moving and competitive.

But when we would ride trails at home, Elvis didn't understand why I wanted him to slow down and sometimes walk behind others. Like for instance the time Marilyn and her friend, Karen, decided to move out towards the trailer at a goodly clip. I never let Elvis trot or canter back to the trailer because it had taken me so long to teach him to slow down and walk to it. As they moved off, I kept the reins tight, telling Elvis he couldn't run after them. Down went his head, and a few bucks later, the discussion came to an end. Even then he still pranced and pulled on the bit all the way back. I was very frustrated until I thought it over. To Elvis, it wasn't fair to ask one thing in the ring and another on the trail. I would have to remember that anything I taught him or allowed him to do at the show would transfer over to our trail rides at home. I couldn't expect him to know the difference.

I found that during training my younger horses, they had to be introduced slowly to things that might scare them. I didn't always remember this when handling Elvis. Since he was older, I would forget there might be things he had not encountered . . . such as elephants.

During a show in Moses Lake, Washington, a traveling circus was camping near the far end of the stall barns at the fairgrounds we were staying at. It seemed that their elephants and ponies didn't have the proper traveling papers to be able to cross the border into Canada.

As I led Elvis down to the wash racks, he spied the movement of the huge pachyderms. Their handlers let them out into a fenced holding area during the day. Elvis took in a deep breath, arched his neck, snorted and started prancing.

I don't know how many times I had laughed at the picture Elvis made out in the pasture. He looked very much like a chunky, little mustang. A passerby would never guess that he could be a classy-looking show horse. I also thought that with his temperate spirit, he would have made a gentle stallion. He changed that opinion.

With a loud snort, he sucked in more air, expanding his already wide chest. Pulling on the lead rope, his nostrils flared wide, and he brought up his tail in a tall plume. Pawing the ground, his dark, expressive brown eyes now had a glint of fire to them. Suddenly my unassuming-looking little Fox Trotter grew about two feet taller and gained about a hundred pounds.

He gave a shrill whinny as he challenged the big gray beasts. They did not respond but continued to sway, tossing dust over their backs. I could barely hold Elvis as he circled around me. Sending challenge after challenge to these beasts, his blood was running hot. I saw the stallion he would have made--and was thankful that he was a gelding. I would never have been able to handle the fiery beast that was at the end of my lead rope.

When the elephants didn't respond to him, he must have thought that dragging me to safety was the next logical step. Doing his ever-favorite maneuver of running through his shoulder, he kept an eye on those hideous beasts as he started to angle towards the safety of his stall.

Jane, who met up with us at the show, thought I was crazy when I wanted to show her and Darrell how Elvis reacted to the elephants. She thought I was even crazier when I suggested we take the horse she was working with, Mellow, down there to introduce him to the elephants. She firmly told me no way would she ride Mellow if I did that.

The circus left the next day, but every time I had to take Elvis down to the wash racks, he'd puff up, snorting, looking for his nemesis, those menacing pachyderms.

Just as I taught Elvis, so he taught me. One of my lessons occurred at the Show and Celebration in Ava, Missouri. Jane warned me several times that when I tied Elvis's lead rope to the trailer, next to the tack room, I was leaving it too long. She would tell me once, maybe twice, not to do something. If I didn't listen, she would then step back and allow me to make the mistake, and if I suffered the consequences of my actions, so be it.

Elvis knew I kept the treats in the tack room. If the rope was too long, he would start rooting around, pulling tack out in search of the horse treats. I was changing in the back of the trailer and could hear a commotion going on in the tack room. I hollered for Jane, who was taking care of Sherman, my other horse. I could hear her come around the back of the trailer, and then she chuckled.

"Elvis, I'm going to let your owner clean this one up. Maybe she will learn to shorten your lead rope."

I came out and around the back of the trailer. There on the ground were bridles, buckets, curry combs and anything else he could get his teeth on, lying strewn about. Growling under my breath, I did indeed learn to tie him short. Sometimes I felt Elvis was a better teacher than I was.

THE HEART OF ELVIS

Chapter Seventeen – Elvis and Elvis

"Well, folks," the announcer drawled, "it looks like Elvis has left the barn!"

Elvis and I would hear this many times through the show season. People always laughed. With a name like Elvis, there was plenty to live up to. But at times you need to be careful, or the joke can be on you. That is exactly what happened to me when I came up with a costume idea.

In the shows I had previously attended, I

noticed they had a costume class. My overactive brain started working on an idea: with a horse named Elvis, I could have Elvis riding Elvis. I ran it by my husband, who agreed it would be fun. I got online and began searching for the perfect outfit. There were scores of costume sites and soon, I found the perfect one, along with the perfect wig, sunglasses, sideburns and sash. It was white, bespectacled with large, fake jewels, a wide sash, bell-bottoms and a cape.

Once the outfit was hanging in my closet, I realized that Elvis would also need a cape. I went to work sewing on sequins, a collar to match my sash, and created an oversized version of my own cape for Elvis. I would put the collar around his neck; the rest of the white cape would cover the saddle and drape over his rump. A sign was made to attach to his breast collar, and I bought a tube of hair gel, which when applied to his mane and forelock, created huge, stiff pin curls. We were quite a sight.

Under the wig and behind the glasses, I could easily become an Elvis impersonator. When I entered the Costume Class for the first time, the club thought we had hired an impersonator to ride Elvis. Several of them were quite shocked to find out it was me under the wig and glasses.

When he moved, the cape flowed like the trappings on an Arabian horse. He acted like he knew he was on display for the crowd. We brought smiles to everyone who saw us. My granddaughter carried on the tradition later when she went into a class dressed as a hippie, proclaiming to be Priscilla and Elvis. He fox-trotted out with that cape flapping in the breeze and never lost the cadence of the trot.

I wanted to retire the Elvis costume, but my family and husband wouldn't hear of it. One summer, Darrell tried talking me into being in the 4th of July Pioneer Parade. I had ridden Elvis in the parade before, so I knew he could handle the commotion, but dressed as Elvis, my ability to handle any emergency situation would be slightly hindered. The grandchildren joined Grandpa in the pleading, so I made a compromise with them. They would have to be in the parade as well. It was decided: Darrell would follow me in his dad's 1941 Chevy filled with the grandkids.

The day was bright and hot, perfect for a parade. Moving out behind the float we were assigned to ride behind, I discovered that Elvis didn't like water balloons. As one splatted near his feet, he skittered on the asphalt. I dismounted quickly. My outfit had huge, bell-bottomed pant legs that drug on the ground. I had to be careful walking beside him, as occasionally he'd step on a pant leg, causing me to stumble and almost lose the pants. So hitching it up at the waist and leading Elvis by the reins, we continued on down the road. During a delay, I grabbed my youngest grandchild, Lindynn, from the car and put her up on Elvis, hoping he would settle down for a grandkid. He did a sniff at the shoe and moved out slowly. Lindynn was only three at the time, but was the most horse-crazy child I had ever seen.

A few minutes later, even after my pleas, another water balloon splatted in front of us. It pushed

Elvis past the edge of calmness. He held still long enough for me to get Lindynn off, and then he started prancing. For another four blocks, I worked between leading Elvis, trying to keep from tripping on my bell-bottoms and losing my pants while smiling and waving at the crowd.

The final ending to the holiday was the next Monday's local newspaper. There on the front page of the Lander Journal, to my utter surprise and chagrin, was a picture of a grimacing Elvis impersonator and a beautiful, gray horse. The article noted that the judges were surprised to find it was a female doing the impersonating. And on top of that, Elvis and I had won 2nd place in the parade!

My favorite memory of Elvis and Elvis is of the 2011 Show and Celebration. Jane, my trainer and best friend, cajoled me into riding as Elvis and Elvis for one last time. My granddaughter spent several days drawing a guitar on a stiff piece of cardboard and then decorated it so I could carry it in the class.

Missouri has high humidity, and the polyester outfit didn't breathe well. I also didn't have Elvis wear his cape due to the moisture and heat. For a change, we didn't draw too many stares. Into the ring we went, and Elvis did what he did best: fox-trot under any circumstance, whether in sagebrush or in high heat and humidity.

As I waited in the lineup while the judges made their decision, my extremely good hearing picked up on their conversation.

"Yeah, I like the Elvis dude. Anyone know

who that guy is?"

Another judge answered him, "The horse is named Elvis also, and that isn't a dude--it's a woman!"

I was glad that I wore original 1980 sunglasses that covered half my face as I watched five judges turn and stare at Elvis and me. We won second place, much to my chagrin, and just for the record, the outfits that the real Elvis wore are definitely not my style!

THE HEART OF ELVIS

Chapter Eighteen
The Feel of Horsemanship

How do you teach someone to ride a horse? Even with the best communication, it is hard to get your views across to another human being, let alone to an animal. Imagine how hard it would be if you couldn't talk but could only communicate through pushing, pulling or pointing someone in the direction you want them to go

It took a long time for me to learn it was not just about a cue--like put the leg on now, lift a rein here. Those were just the mechanics. Elvis was not a machine. I had to learn to ride by a "feel." When you ride a bike, do you think about all the things you are doing or are you looking ahead, just "feeling" the balance, steering and pedaling?

Riding is very much like that. You look ahead, keep your balance, think of what you want and back it up with a subtle cue. For a long time, my riding was very mechanical, not the smooth, unthinking feel of riding. Experience was the only way to learn. Hours in the saddle and trying to teach someone else finally brought home to me what "feel" was all about.

When I let the grandchildren compete with Elvis, I would hear that I had given them a "push-button" horse. That meant Elvis just knew what to do, despite their lack of knowledge, and would go out and do it like a trained circus horse. I knew better. Elvis was not easy to ride.

During the Great Western Celebration, I ran across a girl named Stephanie. The first time we met, her big brown eyes were filling with tears of frustration. We'd just finished Amateur Reining and for the first time since we had started competing in this class, I felt good about the run Elvis and I had made. But Stephanie had struggled. In fact, for two days, her little mare Delilah had been a ball of energy. Stephanie was one of those naturally talented riders, and the mare had put all her skills to the test.

Though she was in the Youth division, she'd decided to try the Amateur Classes, trying to wear out her fiery mare. Now, she was tired and very disappointed. I could see her confidence slipping down her cheek in each crystal tear.

I leaned over Elvis's neck, catching her attention. "It's okay. Elvis and I, just recently, in the middle of the pattern, had to quit. Judge thought I was nuts." A slow smile appeared on her tear-streaked face.

"Really? I just don't know why Delilah is being such a rip. She's usually so good," she said softly.

"I don't know which is worse. A horse that goes too fast or one that goes too slow! Elvis doesn't like Reining. I have to practically get off and push him," I said.

She giggled, and I was relieved. One more tear from those big, baby browns and I was going to become a puddle myself. She kept working through Delilah's energetic performances until, by the last day, she had begun to actually place first in the classes.

A year later, sadly, Delilah was in dire health, having hung up a foot in a corral panel. During the first show of the season, I saw Stephanie sitting out classes while her best friend, Abby, competed.

It was Jaquelynn's second year on Elvis, but her class list was light. Ranch Classes were coming up-- something all the kids really liked to do. Chasing cows was more fun than work. Jaquelynn was too young to work them yet; she still needed practice. But I overheard Stephanie wishing out loud that she could have participated in the Ranch Classes.

I don't know why--maybe it was the memory of those tearful brown eyes or my pride in how well Elvis could perform; either way, I offered to let her do a Ranch Class on Elvis. Her eyes lit up.

"Really? I would love that! He's such a neat horse. I can't believe you'd let me ride him."

I gave her a crash course on cues for Elvis and warned her, "He knows what to do; just let him do it. No ropes though. He hates them."

She nodded enthusiastically, and off she went. Elvis and Stephanie worked their cow, got it into the pen and placed. After an ecstatic "thank you" and hugs, we went home to wait for the next show.

During the Big Sky Missouri Fox Trotter Show, Stephanie was riding another mare but asked if she could ride Elvis during the Ranch Classes. I thought this would be a great workout for Elvis--he needed it. We agreed, but Stephanie was having trouble with Elvis's walk. I had tried telling her the cues but decided it would be easier if I got on the horse and explained the cues as I did them.

"I just keep my hands down and if I feel him start to slow down, I tap with my legs. If he gets rough or speeds up too much, all I do is flick my wrist like this and tuck his nose ever so slightly," I instructed.

It is hard to tell someone the cues that you do on a "feel." You're not conscious of all the fine adjustments. Feeling Elvis shift under me, I'd adjust my own body to communicate and redirect. He'd compensate in response. Up to this point, I had not realized how much interaction was going on to keep

Elvis balanced and in gait.

"I don't see you doing this when you ride. Elvis and you look so smooth," Stephanie said.

I laughed. "Well, good, but trust me: you are talking like crazy up here to him. There is no such thing as a 'push-button' horse."

Ranch Classes went late into the night. I trusted Stephanie, as did Elvis, obviously. They had been doing well together all afternoon. So I decided to go to bed, letting Stephanie put Elvis in his stall for the night.

The next morning she gave me an enthusiastic hug and opened the black velvet box she held. Nestled in the blue satin was a gleaming belt buckle. "High Point Ranch Youth Champion" was stamped boldly across its shiny surface.

"Really? You did that without the Roping Class? I'm impressed."

She looked at me in puzzlement. "No, I did Roping. In fact," she said and looked down shyly, her toe stubbing at the grass, "I won it, but I roped his head."

"What! And he didn't buck with you? Was he skittish?" Again those big brown eyes looked back at me quizzically.

"No. Did I do something wrong?"

"No, I guess not. Elvis just has always acted up around ropes. Darn him. He will do things for you guys he'd never do for me!" I was irritated. Definitely, that horse and I had a love/hate relationship. Then it dawned on me what she had said.

"Did you say you roped his head?" I said in disbelief.

She giggled and explained. "Well, I had too big of a loop, and Elvis--he just knew which cow we needed to cut out, so we had lots of time. When I went to swing, it just went over his head and caught on his ear. But he let me lean forward on his neck and get it off, and then I had another chance to rope my cow."

I hugged her, relieved that Elvis had kept his head, literally.

At the next show, Stephanie finally joined the club of Love/Hate Elvis. During a Trail Class, she had to pick up a canter at the top of the arena and come down around in front of the gate. As Stephanie got him into a beautiful canter, she found out his number-one rule as he ran straight to the gate, crow-hopping as she tried to turn him off of it. They went on to complete the pattern and she still won second place, despite his little detour. Even through all of this, she still remains a loving fan.

Time and again I had watched my instructors get my horses to do a maneuver I could not seem to accomplish. Elvis proved what I had already suspected. It was the rider and their ability to communicate through feel that made the difference. Only the horse--and how it responded–would let me know if I'm a horseman.

I realized my childhood dream of finding a horse to ride off into the sunset with was only in the movies. In real life, it came with a heck of a lot of work!

ROBYNN GABEL

GREAT WESTERN
CELEBRATION
MISSOURI FOX TROTTER SHOW
Sponsored by Utah Foxtrotting Horse Association
JUNE 22-24, 2006

Chapter Nineteen – Arriving

From the moment I watched my friend Peg ride the first Trail Class, my entire goal had been to become a better horseman. Winning first in Trail, I thought, would prove that. I had no idea it would take ten years to accomplish.

In the first full summer of showing, I entered a Trail Class in Hamilton, Montana. I had intensely studied the pattern the night before. There was a complex side-pass obstacle that had me concerned.

Next morning, as I started the class at the gate, Elvis tried to help by pushing it open with his shoulder rather than allowing me to open it. We struggled. Under my breath, I grumbled, "Knock it off, Elvis." I saw a slight smile go across the judge's face. Great, I thought. I wondered how much I would get marked down for cussing at my horse!

We came to the box with the slanted poles on the other side of it. The dreaded side pass was before us. Focused, I headed him through the box. With just pressure from my legs and gentle direction on the reins, we flawlessly executed the maneuver.

The crowd clapped loudly. I noticed that the judge had a frown, but I didn't care. I was elated, until I got outside of the arena. My husband explained I had forgotten to do the 360 pivot in the box. I was heartbroken. I realized it wasn't the horse--it was the rider.

I sat on Elvis, brooding. In the sweltering heat, I made a mental note that a black leather vest and cowboy hat probably weren't the smartest outfit, even if it did complement Elvis's coloring. I reminded myself glumly that remembering a pattern would gain me more points than making a stylish fashion statement.

My husband tried to lighten the mood. "I wonder if the 'H' stands for the town's name of Hamilton.

With narrowed eyes, I glanced up at the

mountainside and growled, "No. It stands for 'hotter than hell.'" Wisely he decided to see what Jane was doing.

They called us back into the arena to receive our places. I was not surprised to get last place. The normally-taciturn judge came up to speak to me while we waited.

"Darn it, I wanted to give you that first-place ribbon. That's the best side pass I've seen out here all day. Study your pattern better the next time." I nodded, gritting my teeth behind my stiff smile.

Besides staying on pattern, I longed for the communication that would make it a dance between my horse and me. Horsemanship, to me, was about the rider-horse team being of one mind, one spirit and one body. It finally happened, only on the wrong horse.

Throughout the years of showing, I also competed on my younger, upcoming horses. I had worked with Mellow for two years. Elvis was now helping to train the grandchildren. I looked over the pattern the night before, chuckling. It looked like someone had taken the most difficult obstacles out of the book, linking them all together. It would be the hardest Trail Class I ever encountered. Mellow picked up on my nervousness much quicker than Elvis, getting anxious himself. But I decided to try it; we needed the practice.

While waiting for the judge's nod the next morning, I took a big breath. The signal came. We opened the gate with smooth precision. Pretending we were at home just practicing, I softly touched his side and suddenly— we were dancing. I looked ahead to each obstacle, thinking how to do it. He responded, reading my body cues. He didn't click a rail or hesitate to back up, flowing with grace, until the last obstacle when I got nervous. Even then, he clicked only one rail.

I came out of the class feeling that, for the first time in my life, I had arrived. Even when, to my utter surprise, we won the class, the blue ribbon wasn't important. Well, not on that horse, anyway.

We were on a two-week circuit of shows. At the next show, I decided to ride both horses in Trail, just for fun. Unbeknown to me, the same judge, who, in my first year of showing, had wanted to give Elvis and me first in Trail, was the show judge.

This time I was faced with a difficult obstacle. It was made up of three barrels that formed a triangle called the "keyhole." I wasn't worried. From opening the gate, crossing the bridge, taking a left lead canter and flatfoot walking around poles, I would think of the moves needed, and my dance partner, Elvis, would follow easily. It was exhilarating.

Now we stopped at the last obstacle, the "keyhole." Exact positioning was the first step. We backed up slowly, rhythmically between two barrels. I continued to think back up, but now, Elvis had to curve around the third barrel that formed the top of the triangle. We kept backing, Elvis stepping lively, knowing exactly what I wanted. Coming out between the two barrels, we hadn't cut it too close or made it too wide, and we hadn't touched any of the barrels.

133

With a graceful turn on the hindquarter, we were done. In a trail walk we headed to the gate to the sound of shouts and clapping.

When the winners were called, the judge handed me the prized first-place ribbon himself, with a smile, saying, "Finally. It's about time. Best keyhole pattern of the bunch."

Tears streamed down my face as I hugged Elvis. All the competitors who had watched my growth over the years were delighted to share in my joy. All the persistence, the lessons, the practice and callouses culminated with two great rides I would never forget.

That night, lying on my bed in the camper, looking up at the long-awaited blue ribbon, I realized that winning a Trail Class didn't prove my horsemanship. It had been the journey that gave me the degree of horsemanship I had always yearned for.

ROBYNN GABEL

Chapter Twenty – The Last Show

"Hey, is that your horse over there on the lawn?"

"No, it's not. I wouldn't own anything that ugly."

I heard them chuckling. Jaquelynn and I were inside the horse trailer, changing clothes. We knew there was only one horse they could be talking about: Elvis.

Across the parking lot was a lawn with the first tender shoots of grass coming up. You'd think Elvis would be happy with a clean stall and nice green hay in his feeder, but no, he'd been looking over at that lawn all day.

136

"I thought I asked you to lock that stall door?" I questioned.

Jaquelynn shot back, "I wasn't the last one out."

We'd just finished putting Elvis in the stall after bathing, clipping, braiding and putting on a fluorescent yellow zebra-striped slinky and a purple horse blanket. I had to agree that it wasn't flattering. Though if they could have seen the picture a professional photographer had gotten of him the year before and won acclaim for, they wouldn't have thought it was the same horse!

Always alert to opportunities, Elvis had taken advantage of my negligence. As I went to get my wayward steed, the hollow-sounding voice of the announcer reverberated from the outside loudspeakers, "Someone's horse is loose. Last I heard, he was heading to McDonalds!"

So began the show season of 2011. As usual, due to chronic back issues, I was on restrictions. I had this nagging feeling that Elvis and I were running out of time. I'd never thought we'd go back to Ava, Missouri, but I had an itch to do so now. Even though, at eighteen, Elvis was still performing at peak levels, I worried that my health issues would soon keep me from riding at all. I decided to just let things play out that summer, before I made up my mind.

Riding in English attire was almost my undoing at the second show of the season. Elvis could have taken full advantage of my lack of confidence in this riding discipline, but didn't. Unfortunately, English

Pleasure was one of the classes required in the Versatility Pleasure circuit. I hated the way English clothing restricted my movements. I felt very much like a tin soldier. Jane still cracks up, remembering the first time she saw me waddle out of the trailer in my new, black wool coat, skin-tight breeches and tall boots.

At this show I had a tight schedule between a Western and English Class. The saddle and bridle had to be switched out. I also needed to change into English clothes. I jumped off Elvis and threw the reins to the grandkids. They went to work on Elvis while I jumped into the back of the trailer to dress. Red-faced and huffing, I tried to pull on the skin-tight breeches in ninety-degree heat. This gets a little sticky, especially when you discover they aren't your pants, but your granddaughters'. I suddenly realized that I had forgotten mine at home. Now I had a dilemma.

Thank heavens those pants were stretchy, but they barely covered my rear end, and zipping them up was not going to happen. Thank heavens the English riding coats are made to hang over the derrière. I stepped out, impressed that the kids had the tack all changed and had a step stool ready for me. It is very hard to get into an English saddle from the ground without a boost and, had the stool not been there, I would have definitely mooned the entire crowd.

As we came into the arena at a trot, I was praying that things would go smoothly. Elvis felt the stiffness that the restricting clothes created as I rode. I gripped hard to balance and stay on that tiny, slick saddle with no horn. He was slow and consistent in his shift from canter to walk to trot. This was good because it made it look like I was keeping him collected and he was following my directions. I hate to admit it--he was just trying to help keep me from falling off.

I hoped no stray breeze would come through and lift the back of my coat, or the audience was going to get more than they wanted. Elvis was a gentleman, smoothly transitioning into all of his gaits and gratefully, I stayed on. The blue ribbon wasn't appreciated nearly as much as my being able to change back into pants that fit.

By the end of the summer show circuit, Elvis had performed so well that we won a belt buckle at the Great Western Celebration for high point in Amateur Versatility Pleasure. This was a new division created for those who could not do Barrels, chase cows, or participate in any other class that required a lot of speed. It was definitely designed for a team like Elvis and me.

Elvis also earned us another belt buckle in the Intermountain Regional Circuit as well. These are won at the end of the show in different high-point divisions. I had coveted a belt buckle because Jane and Jaquelynn had won several of them while competing with my horses. Originally I had laughed at them. Who wanted a belt buckle as a trophy? To me, belt buckles, though nice, were not a practical item. But it had begun to prick my pride that my granddaughter had three of them, all won while riding Elvis . . . the same horse I had ridden and tried so hard to win even a blue ribbon on!

I decided that after this, we were ready for Ava once again. Our second trip back was a little more somber, but no less fun. I knew this was our last show together.

Pulling into the MFTHBA showgrounds in Ava, Missouri, I felt a flutter of excitement. Elvis and I had trained for many years for this moment. As I was signing in, checking over the classes, I was asked if I would like to carry the Wyoming flag for the flag ceremony at the Show and Celebration. I agreed to do it.

Some horses can't tolerate the stimulation of a flag flapping as you ride along, but Elvis didn't mind. Gripping the flagpole with one hand and resting the end of it against the stirrup, I reined Elvis in with my other hand. Off we went in a proud line behind the other representatives. Elvis picked up his fox-trot, his rhythmic head shake creating a flaring wave of black mane. The breeze lifted the flag, the fabric snapping crisply in the air. I felt the ripple of power from his shoulders as he moved his front legs out, reaching for more of the track. My heart pounded with pride while my eyes swelled with tears.

The next day, under the golden haze of sunshine, I sat on Elvis, waiting patiently for the Amateur Western Pleasure Class. I thought back over the years and realized this had been the first class Elvis and I had ever won. Now, we were competing on a Grand-Champion level. In the warm humid air, we entered the arena for our turn. Elvis moved off smoothly. Every time they called a transition, it seemed that fate put us right in front of the judge. Elvis didn't miss one step. The announcer called for a stop; I leaned back, dropped my hands and felt Elvis shifting his speed, sliding his back feet under him. The perfect stop.

The hollow voice over the speaker called for a "trail walk," and Elvis, who by now had learned all the calls and what they meant, lowered his head and slowly started walking alongside the rail. At about the fourth transition call, I glanced over to see the judge smiling. I don't think he could believe our luck either, but it didn't matter.

In all my years of competition, I'd never had the perfect ride. That's where the horse and you do exactly everything spot-on. Not one missed cue, not one missed lead change or gait change. It was our best ride ever. Of course, we also won first, giving us a Grand Champion title.

Again and again we danced through the classes. Elvis did the perfect pivot in Showmanship, and I remembered the pattern, again winning us first. However, in the Performance Ring at the front of the showgrounds, we were struggling. Like an old married couple, I was in tune to his moods. I began to feel a subtle shift in Elvis. Even though he knew his job and did it, there was less willingness to go through the gate. I had threatened to retire him for several years, but the kids and my infirmities kept bringing him back.

The heat had let up. The evening was fairly cool for our first Performance Class. I felt Elvis lean into his shoulder to try and duck out the gate. I corrected it before it happened. Going counterclockwise around the arena was his favorite way. He moved with his tail flowing and his head bobbing. I sat back and enjoyed the ride. Unlike a regular trot, a fox-trot was different and I didn't have to work to keep from being jarred. His flatfoot walk was powerful and smooth. You could sit there and drink tea and not spill a drop.

Then the call came for a reverse: turning around and going clockwise on the track. The battle was on. Finally, it happened in the backstretch . . . a total breakdown. He wouldn't pick up a fox-trot. Prancing along, bowing his neck, none of my cues seemed to work. Of course, I was so stiff, tight and embarrassed, that the cues probably made no sense. I had only wanted a good ride, not necessarily a ribbon.

Elvis was clearly done. He had gone around in circles long enough. I slowed down near the gate and asked to be let out. The gatekeeper was a tall, distinguished-looking man, dressed in a western-cut suit. In his eyes, I read understanding of my frustration and embarrassment.

"Ma'am, they just called the class to the center. If you just want to wait it out there, I'd appreciate it. Otherwise, I have to get permission to let you out. The class is over anyway." I nodded, tears pooling in my eyes. Of course, there were ten horses, and we placed last. This allowed us to ride in the World Grand Champion Class the next night. I didn't care. I just wanted out of the ring. To ride against the best and to have failed so miserably in my communication with Elvis was the height of embarrassment.

In a long talk with Jane, she pointed out that Elvis had been babysitting grandkids through the summer. It wasn't fair for me to expect the communication level to snap right back. I thought it was more than that--he was pushing the boundaries. We practiced late that night.

The next morning, I decided that if we went into the practice ring and couldn't maintain communication, I would cancel the last class. I had promised him retirement; it seemed he was calling me on it. As I rode out, the fall foliage coloring all the trees around us, I relaxed and just enjoyed being with my friend. He readily accepted my requests.

Through the years, his color had changed, as grays will do. Now he had a silver-white coat, a black mane and a little black still on his legs. His coat glistened in the sunlight as he elegantly moved out. His fox-trot beat a cadence that I loved to listen to. For a moment, it was just a girl and her horse, enjoying a pleasant, morning ride. I decided we would try one more ride in the front ring at the Show & Celebration. I wanted to end on a fairy-tale note.

Being the last day of the show, all the final awards were being given out. Bittersweet tears threatened to fall down my face as I accepted the World Grand Championship in Versatility Pleasure. We had placed reserve in overall Amateur Versatility as well.

But the award I treasured over all else was the retirement plaque Elvis's many friends had made for him.   Through the years, he had impressed many judges. They loved coming back from our shows out west and comparing Elvis's stories. One of those judges, with the help of his wife and another judge, had put together a beautiful frame with pictures of Elvis set over an Elvis Presley record.

Elvis was well known in the Western Regional Associations from eight years of competition. The members from those clubs who were there at the Show & Celebration joined in the retirement ceremony. Our MFTHBA Area Representative, Dennis, made the retirement plaque presentation to Elvis. He was also Maddy's father and had appreciated Elvis's sweetness towards her. I didn't know about it until called into the arena for the presentation. Looking around at all the smiles on so many faces, I realized--through the tears in my eyes--Elvis's legacy wasn't in the trophies or the ribbons he collected but in the many hearts he had touched.

Along with the plaque was a twelve-page printout from Donna, the secretary in the front office, showing all the classes Elvis had ever participated in. Looking at those twelve pages, all those long years of classes, it hit home once again: it was time. I was surprised at how many gates he had gone out of and arenas he had circled, showing off and patiently trying to please. And this didn't include all the practice we had done.

That evening, because Elvis had been inconsistent in the previous classes, I knew we didn't stand a chance of placing. But I had to erase the memory of the ride the night before. I knew we could do better than that. As we warmed up, waiting for our class, I felt a sense of melancholy. It had been a way of life for eight years, spending so much time with my best friend as we worked towards my goals.

I took a big breath. The gate opened; the lights shone brightly. The crowd started cheering for their individual favorites. Trainers and friends called from the stands, encouraging the twelve horses sweeping onto the track. The sound of their hoofs in the fox-trot cadence mingled with the beat of the song the organ player created.

The cool evening air pushed against us. Elvis trotted out, surging to pass the horse on the track in front of him. Mane flying, ribbons jumping to his rhythmic head shake, his hoofs beating out the familiar pattern. It was perfect. They called the reverse, and I relaxed. Remembering Jim from the first Show & Celebration telling me, "He knows what to do." My hands held the reins lightly. I trusted he would go into the fox-trot, and he did. I smiled all the way around, enjoying an evening ride with my friend.

I knew it might not have been noticed by anyone else, but my smile was full of the knowledge that Elvis and I had accomplished the perfect last ride together. And it was better than any ribbon, trophy or belt buckle ever won, when Rick, the tall gatekeeper of the night before, lifted his cowboy hat, giving me a smile and a gentlemanly nod as we left the ring.

In the long drive home from Ava, I realized it wasn't the showing itself, but the riding it took to get there, that had fulfilled my dream of becoming a horseman. But the ride wasn't over. It wasn't the end of the trail yet.

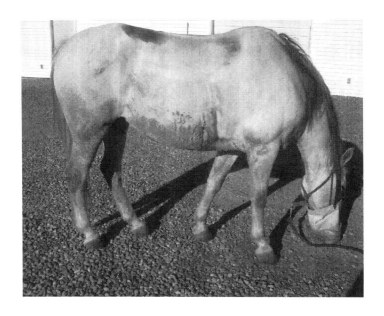

Chapter Twenty One – Happily Ever After

Elvis's show days were over. The first-place ribbon for Trail was in a shadow box along with the gate sheet that everyone had signed in congratulations. It hung on the wall next to his retirement plaque. He had nothing to do but spend hours chomping on green grass. Even so, he didn't seem content. Coming to the gate, he'd watch as we loaded the other horses in the trailer for excursions to trail rides or training in the arena. He'd toss his head and trot down the fence as we would pull out, unhappy to be left behind.

I had been thinking. Even if his show days were over, there were still trail rides we could do. I had done some research on the American Competitive Trail Horse Association. I found that they had competitive, six-mile rides with obstacles. Their whole focus was helping people find jobs for their rescue horses, rehabilitated mustangs or older horses.

This would be different for Elvis. It wouldn't be mind-numbing circles but new adventures on new trails. I had helped in the show circuit; I saw no reason why I couldn't set up an ACTHA ride in my own area. That meant I would have to find six miles of trail with natural obstacles. Elvis and I had a new job. There had been one area in particular I was scouting. We had to do many hours of riding to check it out.

I was on my last obstacle. I needed a water crossing. I called my friend Peg, and she agreed to ride with me. Elvis was happy to be loaded into the trailer. He knew he was going to get a fresh hay bag to munch on while we traveled. It was a beautiful, late-spring day. The area we were riding in was surrounded by red cliffs, scrub pine and many little arroyos and hills. It was peaceful and idyllic.

Twin Creek was a small, meandering stream that ran up against a limestone ridge. It pooled behind the rock, spilling over into another small pool, then flowed out across the prairie. In the heat of the day, the horses had worked up a little sweat. As Peg and I talked, Elvis stepped into the pool to grab a quick drink.

"I don't think this is a good place to cross--it's very narrow, and on the other side, it's muddy," I said.

Peg looked up at the top of the falls. "I wonder

if we can get up there. I'm pretty sure there is a trail around the rock cropping there." She took the lead, and Elvis and I followed her. Sure enough, at the top of the ridge, there was a large pool.

I must explain about water and me. There are fears and then there are phobias. I didn't fear water....I was terrified of bodies of water. As long as I can touch bottom with my feet, then I can stay sane. The minute I can't, an unexplainable terror seizes me. That's the best way I can describe it. I've told all my family and friends: if I fall into a body of water, do not come in after me. Just let me drown because otherwise, I will drown you.

The pool was wide and looked inviting in the warmth of the day. Elvis wanted another drink, so I dropped the reins—trusting him--because after all, he knew what he was doing, right? He walked out onto the muddy bank and stepped into the water. Suddenly we were in the water with nothing under my feet. There had been a drop-off and Elvis was now swimming.

First, let me tell you the last sane thought that went through my head: Elvis is my flotation device and I am not leaving my flotation device. I wrapped my arms around the saddle horn. To me, the little flow of water over the ledge, which created a gentle falls below, had just become Niagara Falls, and we were being pulled towards it by the rapids rushing all around us. I started screaming.

Peg said she had never seen anyone freak out like I did. Nor had she ever seen a horse do what Elvis did next. He had never heard me scream like that and must have thought I was dying. Whatever went through his mind, he kept his cool, unlike me. Wrenching himself around in the water, he heaved himself up on the muddy bank, sinking his right leg to the chest in the boggy mud, folding his left leg underneath himself. Scrambling with his back feet—still half submerged— he found the edge of the bank. Knowing he could do nothing for now, he noticed the tall, lush grass in front of his nose. Forever the eternal opportunist, he leaned over and started to graze.

Meanwhile, Peg's calm voice cut across the terror haze in my mind. "Robynn, listen to me. He can't get out with you on his back. He's got to work himself out of the mud. I don't have a rope to help him. You are going to have to crawl off of him."

She had to repeat this several times to reach me. I thought we were still in the water, but when I finally looked down, I noticed that my right leg was sunk in mud up to the middle of my calf. My left leg was encased to my ankle. With Peg's quiet, calm voice directing me, I finally unclenched my arms from the saddle horn, raised my left leg and drew it up and out-- with some effort--from the sucking mud.

Next, I went to work trying to get my right leg out. After a struggle and loss of my shoe, I finally was clear and able to crawl off the saddle and across the muddy bar we had stepped onto. Once I was off, Elvis worked to crawl out of the mud himself. It took a few minutes, but finally he stood on solid ground. His saddle was covered in mud. I climbed back on, and we headed home. In my mind, Elvis had just saved me from a near-death experience.

As of the writing of this chapter, Elvis is still a character. I don't know how many more years of stories we have left. All I know is that I've been very blessed to have Elvis choose to share this journey with me.

THE HEART OF ELVIS

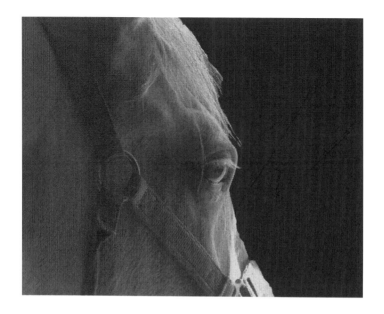

Epilogue

Throughout the years, I have imagined the scene of how Elvis came to Earth, wondering if it went something like this:

Somewhere in Heaven are sweet, lush-green pastures filled with the most exquisite of all creatures: horses. They have glowing, shiny hides and silken manes and tails that float on the slightest breeze.

One day, a call went forth that several special horses were needed down on Earth for some extra-needy humans.

One raised his head. The color of molten silver, with brown eyes full of intelligence, he listened.

Snorting, he went back to grazing. The call came again, louder. They had only one more spot to fill, and it was an especially needy human. Only an exact match would do.

The silver-gray horse sighed, looking around at the field of endless grass. He had to admit: it had gotten a little boring lately, just eating and not doing much of anything but looking dazzling. A little adventure might be nice.

With unearthly power, he floated across the pasture to meet up with St. Peter.

"I will serve," he said, "but I want to be a race horse."

St. Peter's eyes were alight with humor, and smiling, he gently warned, "It will be a most clumsy, stubborn human. You are equally matched. Both of you have heart. Just remember to have patience."

So down to earth went the spirit of Jake's Elvis J.

Acknowledgements:

To write Elvis's story was quite the undertaking as so many have taken part in it. There are many more not listed here to whom I owe my thanks.

Suzanne Scott, Marie Klein, Dan Schurg, Kasey Gabel, Susan Engle and Nikki Shepherd, were gracious enough to read and comment extensively along the way.

Jane Zubia and my ever patient husband were the ones most put upon as they spent hours listening to re-write after re-write.

Then there was Rick Carufel who worked diligently to combine pictures with manuscript as well as create copy after copy of the book cover to find just the right combination to fill that elusive dream of mine on what it should look like.

Without a doubt though, the driving, defining force behind any writer, is the unfailing editor. I have one that is working towards sainthood. I have been so blessed to be able to work with Chryse Wymer. Without her discerning eye, feel for plot, and ever gentle persistence, this story would not be half as good. And forever my grateful thanks to my best friend and humble subject of my story, Jake's Elvis J.

64437695R00090

Made in the USA
Charleston, SC
27 November 2016